THE
HUMAN
SITUATION

by Harvey Jackins

Revised Edition

RATIONAL ISLAND PUBLISHERS

Seattle

First printing, September	1973
Second printing, February	1974
Third printing, February	1975
Fourth printing, February	1976
Fifth printing, April	1977
Sixth printing, November	1978
Seventh printing, April	1980
Eighth printing, January	1983
Ninth printing, April	1988
Tenth printing, April	1989

Revised edition

First printing, April	1991
Second printing, May	1995
Third printing, October	1998
Fourth printing, June	2002
Fifth printing, September	2010

Manufactured in the United States of America

International Standard Book Number:
Paperback: 0-913937-47-9

Intelligence can count the neighbors' sheep,
Or bore two mountain tunnels so they meet,
Can shrewdly estimate the sun's interior,
Or measure, well enough, galactic atoms
A million parsecs distant.

                              Close at hand
We've had more trouble grasping things that matter.

We've not thought clearly about humans ever
In our recorded or suspected history.
                                    Here,
Where the small group of us, by accident
Were moved to let the healing process flow,
Assisting and not hindering for a change,
Some rifts in this confusion have appeared.

These are rifts only yet. Confusion still
Persists when humans try to think of humans,
But these few insights, though beginnings only,
When checked with mirrors, periscopes, and logic
Are quite worth passing on to one another.

These glimpses can be critical to progress,
Can give one's effort purpose and direction
Much as the handlines staked for mountain traveler
Can guide to safety round the foggy steeps.

CONTENTS

FOREWORD

The basic theory and practice of Re-evaluation Counseling were worked out in the 1950s and '60s in Seattle and were communicated verbally among the Seattle area Co-Counselors. The first general publication of theoretical material came in the middle 1960s.

Rapid growth of the Re-evaluation Counseling Communities began in the late 1960s, not so much in response to the publication of theory as to the personal communication of theory by experienced Co-Counselors who had left Seattle and settled in new localities. Once substantial numbers of people were Co-Counseling away from Seattle, however, a desire for more written theory was insistently expressed.

Theory and practice have continued to develop, and it has been a continuing problem to get this backlog of knowledge and new developments on paper and into wide distribution. The lag has been met to some extent by the informal but wide-ranging discussions of theory in *Rough Notes from Buck Creek I* and *Rough Notes from La Scherpa I*. These are transcripts from early workshops and have been invaluable source books for developing teachers of Re-evaluation Counseling classes. Tape cassettes such as *Introductory Lecture* and the memorable *Affection, Love and Sex at the University of Maine* have also been useful, and many more of these are in preparation. Short articles and pamphlets have been published at intervals. The demand for published material, however, has continued to exceed the supply.

The present volume, *The Human Situation*, contains the short essays and articles that appeared between 1962 and early 1973, with some revision and some new material. Together with *The Human Side of Human Beings* and the *Fundamentals of Co-Counseling Manual*, this book should round out the basic theoretical knowledge necessary for students of Re-evaluation Counseling to become functioning members of the Co-Counseling Communities.

The written word, however, is no substitute for the actual experience of Co-Counseling. Everyone who has learned to use Re-evaluation Counseling has done so by first having a "session," that is, being counseled by an experienced Re-evaluation Counselor, and Re-evaluation Counseling is not something to read about but to use. One-to-one contact will undoubtedly continue to be the basic method of first communication, but once that has been achieved, then the theoretical material in the present volume will be of vital use to developing Co-Counselors, teachers, and Community leaders.

If you, the reader, are not presently in contact with the Re-evaluation Counseling Communities and would like to be, you are most welcome to write to me at 719 Second Avenue North, Seattle, Washington 98109, USA, and I will be happy to put you in touch with the experienced Co-Counselors who are nearest you.

Thanks to the Reference Persons, teachers, and members of the Re-evaluation Counseling Communities, to the counselors and workers at Personal Counselors in Seattle, and to my family for requesting this book and assisting it into print.

—Harvey Jackins
June 15, 1973

Foreword to the
1991 Revised Edition

The "Postulates" of Re-evaluation Counseling were revised in 1990 after much discussion in the Communities. "Multiplied Awareness" and "Allow Ourselves Time to Grow" were revised in 1991 to bring some of their organizational implications up-to-date. Otherwise, this book continues in its classical form, already a part of history, but a living, continuing influence in a growing number of lives.

—Harvey Jackins
April 15, 1991

Foreword to the
2010 Revised Edition

This edition of *The Human Situation* contains only a few, modest changes. This book is a very important source of some of the basic ideas and theory of Re-evaluation Counseling. It is also an important source of historical information on the development of Re-evaluation Counseling's theory and practice. We have updated language in only a few places. We have also added both footnotes and notations to the original articles.

Re-evaluation Counseling continues to develop in both theory and practice. A few of the developments discussed here were used for a period of time and were then superceded by other developments and are now no longer used.

—Tim Jackins
August, 2010

THE
HUMAN
SITUATION

The world today has many brilliant people
Who come to false conclusions with their
        brilliance.
Sometimes their logic falters where a pattern
Of old distress deflects their thinking process
But often they can claim their logic flawless
If they omit to question their assumptions.

So it behooves us, too, to look most sharply
At what *we* start with when we do *our* thinking,
And publish broadly the exact foundations
On which our growing structure is erected.

THE POSTULATES OF RE-EVALUATION COUNSELING[1]

Defini: Re-evaluation Counseling is a theory of human behavior and a set of procedures for solving human problems. It is a complex theory, still growing, containing a large amount of information in its details and techniques. Its main assumptions can be summarized at present (1990) in the following twenty-eight points.

1. Rational human behavior is qualitatively different from the behavior of other forms of life. (It is not just more complicated.)

Adaptive 2. The essence of rational human behavior consists of responding to each instant of living with a new response, created afresh at that moment to precisely fit and handle the situation of that moment as that situation is defined by the information received through the senses of the person (other living creatures typically respond with pre-set, inherited response patterns—"instincts," or with conditioned, equally-rigid modifications or replacements of the inherited response patterns, acquired through experiences of stress).

Intelligent 3. This ability to create new, exact responses may be defined as human intelligence. It operates by comparing and contrasting new information with that already on file from past experiences and constructing a response based on similarities to past situations but modified to allow for the differences.

---

[1] First published in 1964 as a pamphlet; revised in 1990 and appeared in *Present Time* No. 76, July 1990.

Physiological Assump.

4. Each human with a physically undamaged brain has a large inherent capacity for this rational kind of behavior, very large as compared to the best functioning of presently observable adult humans.

Awareness

5. The complexity of our central nervous systems (now estimated to contain at least one-thousand billion individual neurons and a number of possible states of relationship between these neurons larger than the number of atoms in the known universe) has brought us not only human intelligence of a very, very high level but also has conferred on us the capacity to be aware, to notice what is going on while it is going on, to think about the rational processes while they are taking place. This ability or function of awareness is very hard to define or describe, but humans are completely aware when it is present in another person or not, and enjoy it fully in themselves when it is operating.

Decision making capacity

6. This complexity of our central nervous systems has also conferred upon us complete freedom of decision. Even though this freedom is denied unendingly and emphatically by the societies in which we live, it still persists and is completely available to us. This complete freedom of decision is not just freedom to make a good decision, to make a rational decision, to make a correct decision. It is an unfettered freedom. We are completely free to make wrong decisions, destructive decisions, irrational decisions as well. Our freedom of choice is unfettered, unlimited.

Abil. to get desired responses fr universe

7. This complexity has also conferred complete power on each individual, if we define power as the ability to have the universe respond to us in the way we rationally wish it to (not in the usual oppressive society's definition of power as "the ability to enforce our will upon other intelligences, other humans").

Inborn - socially communic enthusiastic

8. The natural emotional tone of a human being is zestful enjoyment of life. The natural relationship between any two human beings is loving affection, communication and cooperation.

9. The special human capacity for rational response can be interrupted or suspended by an experience of physical or emotional distress. When this occurs information input through the senses then stores as an unevaluated and rigid accumulation, exhibiting the characteristics of a very complete, literal recording of all aspects of the incident.

10. Immediately after the distress experience is concluded or at the first opportunity thereafter, the distressed human spontaneously seeks to claim the aware attention of another human. If he or she is successful in claiming and keeping this aware attention of the other person, a profound process of what has been called discharge ensues.

11. Discharge is signalized externally by one or more of a precise set of physical processes. These are: crying or sobbing (with tears), trembling with cold perspiration, laughter, angry shouting and vigorous movement with warm perspiration (tantrum), live, interested talking; and in a slightly different way, yawning, often with scratching and stretching. Discharge requires considerable time for completion.

12. During discharge, the residue of the distress experience or experiences is being recalled and reviewed (not necessarily with awareness).

13. Rational evaluation and understanding of the information received during the distress experience occurs automatically following discharge and only following discharge. It occurs only to the degree that discharge is completed. On completion, the negative and anti-rational effects of the experience are completely eliminated.

14. As a result of long-term conditioning of the entire population, the spontaneous attempt to claim the aware attention of another person and proceed to discharge and re-evaluation is almost always rebuffed. (Don't cry. Be a big boy. Get a grip on yourself. Don't be afraid. Watch your temper.) Applied to small

children, these rebuffs begin and perpetuate the conditioning of the population which prevents discharge.

15. Undischarged and unevaluated recordings of distress experiences become compulsive patterns of behaving, feeling, and verbalizing when restimulated by later experiences which resemble them strongly enough. Under such conditions of re-stimulation the rational faculty of the human is again suspended and the new information of the current experience is added to the rigid distress pattern making it more far-reaching in its effect and more easily restimulated in the future.

16. We have called the association of distress recordings from the past with the current scene, and the resulting rigid, "inap-propriate" responses "restimulation." This kind of association must have been originally a decision, a decision apparently motivated by the hope that bringing up and "restimulating" the distress recordings would create a possibility of discharg-ing them (if the attention of another person could be found or some other contradiction to the recordings could be achieved). The repetitive attempts at this kind of decision and the resulting lack of success (since we seldom found the resource of contra-diction and resulting discharge we hoped for) tended to make restimulation into a "habit" and a pattern.

It is possible (and profitable) to decide not to be restimulated. Such a decision can be repeated as many times as necessary.

17. The effect of an undischarged distress experience record-ing in "playing" the bearer through a compulsive, repetitive re-enactment of distress experiences is an adequate explana-tion for all observable irrational behavior in human beings, of whatever kind or degree.

18. Any human being, and human beings in general, can become free of the restrictions, inhibitions and aberrations of accumulated distress experience recordings by reinstating a relationship with some other person's or persons' aware atten-

tion and allowing the discharge and re-evaluation processes to proceed to completion.

19. Any infant can be allowed to remain free of aberration by protection from distress experiences and by allowing full discharge and re-evaluation on the ones that do occur.

20. Though a greater degree of awareness, rationality, understanding and skill on the part of the person whose attention is used ("the second person," "the counselor") provides for more rapid and more complete discharge and re-evaluation, the process is workable if even a small degree of awareness is available and if even a roughly correct attitude is maintained by the second person.

21. By "taking turns," i.e., by exchanging the two roles periodically ("Co-Counseling"), two people can become increasingly effective with each other and help free each other from accumulated distress patterns to a profound degree.

22. Distress patterns which have become too reinforced by repeated restimulation can become chronic, i.e., surround and envelop all behavior and activity. To discharge these requires initiative, skill, and resource on the part of the second person and considerable time for handling, but they are not different in origin or effect from lighter distresses, and can also be completely discharged and evaluated.

23. Distress experiences result from any unfavorable aspect of the environment. In our present state of civilization, the bulk of early distress experiences of any child result exactly from the dramatized distress recordings of adults which the adults received from earlier generations when they were children. We have a sort of transmission of aberration by contagion here—well-meaning adults unawarely but systematically infecting each new, healthy-to-begin-with child with their burdening distress patterns.

(handwritten margin notes: Society ⇄ indiv; Distress patterns root of all probs; Indiv choose to be rational)

24. The irrationalities of society (enforcements, punishments, exploitations, prejudices, group conflicts, wars) are reflections of the individual human distress patterns which have become fossilized in the society and often enforced by the rigidities of the society itself.

25. No individual human has an actual, rational conflict of interest with another human. No group of humans has an actual, rational conflict of interest with another group of humans. Given rationality, the actual desires of each individual and each group can best be served by mutual cooperation.

26. Nothing prevents communication, agreement, and cooperation between any humans except distress patterns. Given knowledge of their nature, these distress patterns can be coped with, handled, and removed.

27. Any individual or group can act rationally first without waiting for rational action on the part of someone else, and can take control of the situation by so doing.

28. It is always safe to be rational. Knowledge of the above information can be applied to all aspects of living and to all relationships with real profit and success.

Re-evaluation Counseling is a meaningful and useful description of the nature of human beings and the source of their difficulties. It is a rediscovery of the workable means for undoing human distress. It is a system of procedures for expediting this discharge and re-evaluation process. It is a promising and successful alternative to individual and social irrationality and distress.

"Re-evaluation Counseling," as a title, correctly denotes the collection of insights into the actual nature of reality which we have assembled as the result of our practice and thinking, in the areas of human thought and activities where this actual reality has been occluded or undiscovered as a result of lack of information, misinformation, distress patterns, and the operations of the oppressive societies.

A living theory is growing, changing
As long as it is living. None should claim
To be the one expression of the truth
Since each must be conjecture.
                              Even so
A theory which states its own assumptions
And holds to logical consistency
Deserves consideration of itself
For what it really is, not through confusion
With any other system.

THE DISTINCTIVE CHARACTERISTICS OF RE-EVALUATION COUNSELING[2]

I have often been asked by members of lecture audiences to elucidate the differences between Re-evaluation Counseling and other approaches to human behavior. I used to try to do this, but have concluded that it was a mistake, that I will make such attempts no longer. To attempt this requires that I, in a sense, describe these other systems to the audience, and this places me in a false position since I should not really speak for these other theories. Their spokespersons and theoreticians are widely published and the questioner can easily do his or her own research into what each purports to offer.

I do know something about Re-evaluation Counseling, however, and, with hindsight, it seems that this is what my audiences really want to hear anyway. What are the fundamental features of the Re-evaluation Counseling system that are distinct from other approaches? After some thought, and conversations with people both inside and outside of Re-evaluation Counseling, I have assembled a list of what I think these distinctive features are. The list is still growing—perhaps the reader can point out some crucial features which I have missed. At this writing (May 1973) it numbers 35 points. Some of these points are *unique* to Re-evaluation Counseling. As a set, they are *distinctive*.

---

[2] First published in 1973 as a pamphlet.

(1) First, our definition of intelligence is basic. We define human intelligence as the ability to respond to each different situation in the environment with a fresh, new accurate response.

(2) Second, we make a sharp distinction between "feelings" and this intelligence as a guide to action. "Feelings are to be felt" is the guideline. If they are good feelings, enjoy them, but don't be guided by them. If they are bad feelings, feel them and discharge them but don't be guided by them. Logic should always be the guide. Regardless of how one feels, it should always be possible to determine the right thing to do and do it.

(3) Our concept of the basic, underlying integral nature of the human being is primarily based on the assumption of a very large amount of flexible intelligence, of the ability to come up with new, accurate, successful responses for each person with an undamaged forebrain. *The nature of the human is integral, wholesome.* The natural feeling of a human being is zest, the natural relationship with other human beings is love and cooperation. We assume this is the inherent nature. We regard distress as a disfunction rather than as a "bad side." We try to avoid the old dichotomies of yang and yin, good and evil, etc. We regard distress or poor behavior as a disfunction which occurs for definite reasons and about which something can be done.

(4) We assume that the only *source* of disfunction in a human being is an experience of *hurt,* either physical or emotional, which leaves the information input during that hurt experience in the form of a rigid, compulsive pattern of feeling and behavior rather than as useful information.

(5) We assume complete recoverability from distress, provided the forebrain is intact. This is a postulate, an assumption. None of us has completely recovered yet. The fact that it *is* a postulate has a definite influence on each counseling session. A counselor with this attitude takes very different actions than does one with different assumptions.

(6) We set a goal of total function for the human being. We reject any cultural standards of norm and assume that the human being has the capacity to flower and flourish far beyond any presently observable models. We assume that the outstanding abilities which show up in some human beings are latent in everyone, but inhibited. We set the goal of complete flowering of the human being, not simply adjusting to a particular environment or society.

(7) We assume *discharge is* the important and almost the only step in the recovery process that requires outside assistance. By discharge we mean a series of very complex processes that human beings go through that we are not in a position to define physiologically as yet. (We doubt that any physiologist is ready at present.) These processes can be observed to happen. We assume that they are very complex, and we concentrate on what we call the dependable outward indications of these processes: tears, trembling, perspiration, laughter, angry shouting, reluctant but non-repetitive talk, eager talk, and associated with these, the process that is dependably characterized by yawns.

(8) We assume that, given attainable conditions, discharge becomes spontaneous.

(9) We understand that the precondition for successful discharge is the division of the client's free attention approximately equally between the distress on which discharge is being sought and material contradictory to the distress.

(10) The results of discharge are the dissolution of the compulsive pattern, a freeing of the frozen intelligence, and the conversion of the pattern to useful, available and evaluated information.

(11) The organization of the general techniques of Re-evaluation Counseling in a *spectrum arrangement* permits the safe, effective counseling of any individual in any state of distress. This is in practice tempered by the realization that a deeply distressed

person may require enormous resource in order for a good job to be done, and so Co-Counselors must consider carefully their own resources of time and experience before undertaking to help a deeply distressed person. The general rule remains for Co-Counselors to seek new people who will be able to Co-Counsel back successfully after a small preliminary investment.

(12) We assume the possibility and necessity of exhaustive discharge; that for a particular distress, every bit of stored tension can and needs to be discharged.

(13) We assume that the mind has full capacity to heal itself given the opportunity for discharge, and that ingestion of any substances other than adequate nutrition (any drugs that interfere with mental functioning—narcotics, tranquilizers, stimulants, psychiatric drugs, psychedelics, etc.) are harmful and interfere with the recovery process. The use of such drugs is incompatible with Re-evaluation Counseling.

(14) We hold to the concept that the client is in charge of the process of counseling and that the counselor is a necessary but precisely limited helper. The counselor (or the second person) is in a helping position, not in an authoritative position.

(15) Any diagnoses are made by the client, and we regard them as tentative and subject to revision after the next burst of discharge. Counselors do not diagnose. They will make tentative guesses in their own minds and be guided by them in their roles as assistants, but will never impose them on the client.

(16) Re-evaluation Counseling is not regarded as an emergency measure to be ceased on attaining "normalcy." It is regarded as an ongoing process, as a continuing tool for living.

(17) The counselor draws no conclusions for the client. It is expected that the client will do his or her own thinking. The counselor is under an injunction not to let the thinking she or he does be communicated and get in the client's way.

(18) The client is fundamentally self-directing in the counseling process but has a "contract" with the counselor, for the counselor to intervene when the client's distress interferes with the discharge process. Experienced Co-Counselors are very aware of this, and beginning Co-Counselors operate intuitively, but this is always the basic relationship.

(19) We draw a clear distinction between the *person*, good and wholesome in every respect, and the *distress pattern*, which appears to represent the person but which is actually a foreign element, parasitic upon the person.

(20) Making this distinction between pattern and person, we are consistently *validating* towards each other and avoid the common mistake of being critical and invalidating in the name of "truth" or "sincerity."

(21) We are sure that a distinction between aware activity and unaware activity is not the same as a distinction between rational and irrational behavior. A large amount of rational thinking and acting takes place on an unaware level while compulsive behavior can be "faced" and not discharged and still remain irrational.

(22) The peer relationship is crucial in Re-evaluation Counseling. Co-Counseling is two-way, the Co-Counselors taking turns. If A is client and B is counselor at this session, at the next session A is counselor and B is client. The roles are not only reversible but are regularly reversed in this main mode of Re-evaluation Counseling.

(23) We believe that theory should be in full possession of the client as far as possible. The domain of theory is not restricted to the counselor. Co-Counseling works better if the client is the expert.

(24) The ongoing *counseling of the counselor* is important. No one acts as counselor without being counseled. Even a one-way client

who is getting help for a fee from a professional Re-evaluation Counselor has the right to expect that next week the counselor will be in better shape than he or she was last week because the counselor had a session in the meantime. We determined this many years ago from experience—that no one should counsel without being counseled.

(25) The distinction we make between intermittent and chronic distress patterns is important. It took us a long time to clarify the difference between a distress pattern that is triggered now and then and one which operates all the time and encompasses the person and his or her behavior, and the different approaches necessary to free the client from each.

(26) The notion of a full-time direction against a chronic pattern is crucial to success against such a pattern. The client will accept a direction contradicting a distress pattern, making it vulnerable to discharge not only in his or her counseling session but in all of his or her living. He or she will attempt to "starve the pattern to death," to deprive it of its grip on a person's lifestyle by contradicting it and making discharge that much more available in the sessions themselves.

(27) Co-Counselors apply the theory not only in sessions but as a way of life. This aspect has become prominent in the last few years. In workshops and classes where Re-evaluation Counselors meet and discuss, this engages a great deal of their attention and enthusiasm. People try to clean up their lives and live rationally by these principles. Co-Counseling isn't an activity isolated from living.

In our Communities we have people of all occupations. The people with common interests develop great enthusiasm for applying Re-evaluation Counseling theory in their particular fields. Classroom teachers, for example, try to change the present difficult situation in classrooms by the use of validation and support, by allowing children to discharge and setting up Co-Counseling relationships between them.

(28) Use of the theory becomes an ongoing project. People not only broaden use of the theory into all aspects of life, but also plan to extend its use into the future for its impact on future society.

(29) Re-evaluation Counseling spreads mostly by one-to-one communication of theory. Nearly everyone who now participates was recruited on such a one-to-one basis. (Someone experienced gave each of them a session.) A new person begins to really grasp the theory only after he or she has had his or her first session.

(30) Practice is largely communicated on an "each-one-teach-one " basis. Everyone who Co-Counsels is encouraged to teach another individual how to Co-Counsel. He or she doesn't have to get permission. The teachers who teach classes and offer Re-evaluation Counseling to the public require the approval of the Community, but each individual Co-Counselor is encouraged to teach another individual.

(31) Group and Community activities grow inevitably out of the paired Co-Counseling relationship.

(32) Re-evaluation Counseling theory arose out of spectacularly successful *experiences* with solving people's problems. The successes were accidental to begin with, but they occurred. With cautious experimentation they became reproducible as the elements of the situations that had led to the first successes were located and used with other people's problems. As these successful experiences were more and more dependably reproduced, the theory of Re-evaluation Counseling arose as a careful and tentative explanation of why these successes took place and what the dependable elements in the counseling situations were that consistently allowed distressed people to make such rapid gains. The successful experiences came first, and *then* the theory.

(33) The theory of Re-evaluation Counseling grew as an *inductively logical* structure.

The mistake of attempting to explain these successes on the basis of existing confused theories was avoided by an early decision to make a completely fresh start, to include nothing in the developing theory of Re-evaluation Counseling simply because someone had said it was so or wrote a book saying it was so. We (my early associates and I) decided early in the process to be rigorous about restricting the basis of the growing theory to *our own* experiences with the clients that *we ourselves* worked with and to *only* those parts of the experiences that proved consistently reproducible.

(34) Re-evaluation Counseling has a *deductively* logical structure parallel to, and supporting the inductively logical structure which first evolved.

By the early 1960s we had accumulated a large amount of observational information from our work with clients, all of which information pointed in the same general directions. We decided at that point to attempt a deductively logical structure for the theory to complement the inductively logical structure which we had been erecting. At this point we prepared a list of twenty-four assumptions on which the theory was based, and published them as the Postulates of Re-evaluation Counseling. Since that time, new developments in theory have been worked out as theorems consistent with and derived from these assumptions. At the same time, these theoretical propositions continue to be checked against reality through the work of professional Re-evaluation Counselors, through the experience of the increasingly large number of Co-Counselors, and through the experiences of the Re-evaluation Counseling Communities.

There is a clear distinction between a conclusion reached by deductive logic, air-tight and inevitable given the starting premises, and a conclusion reached by inductive logic, by "the weight of the evidence"; that is, reasoning from particular observations to a general conclusion, a process always carrying with it the possibility that one more observation could undermine the generality of the conclusion.

RC logic is precarious

16

The greater rigor of deductive logic is illustrated by a humorous exhibit in the Seattle Science Center which illuminates this difference. It is framed from the viewpoint of the mathematician and his or her purely deductive logic. The exhibit goes:

THE MATHEMATICIAN LOOKS AT OTHER DISCIPLINES

When asked to prove the *false statement*: "All odd numbers are prime"

the physicist answers	Let's see... 3 is prime, 5 is prime, 7 is prime, 9 is... wait, 9 can be divided by 3... but 11 is prime, and 13 is prime. Yes, all odd numbers are prime; 9 must be an experimental error.
the chemist answers	Well, 3 is odd, and it's prime...5 is odd, and is prime... 7 is odd, and it's prime... I guess that's enough data to say that all odd numbers are prime.
the engineer answers	All right, 3 is odd and it's prime, 5 is prime... 7 is prime... 9 is prime... 11 is prime... 13 is prime....
the theologian answers	Yes, 3 is prime. Since that is so, I think we could say that all odd numbers are prime.

---

(35) Re-evaluation Counseling attains and requires logical consistency in its theory and practice and does not borrow from, nor hybridize with other theories and practices, even though there may be superficial similarities to them. Today

(early 1973) Re-evaluation Counseling is receiving a great deal of attention. New people are joining classes and Communities at an explosive rate. Among these new participants are many professional therapists, clinical psychologists and psychiatrists who have become interested, are communicating with us and are participating in Re-evaluation Counseling. Sometimes, out of previous indoctrination, insecurity, or confusion, some new participants (professionals or laymen followers) want to mix or blend the theories and practices of other therapies and psychologies with Re-evaluation Counseling and are puzzled and offended when we firmly insist that they not do so.

(Anyone is free of course to use the *knowledge* of Re-evaluation Counseling which they have acquired in any way their responsible judgment decides, but we insist that they not *call* what they are doing Re-evaluation Counseling when they are mixing it with other practices, and that they not use such a mixture with their Co-Counselors in Re-evaluation Counseling classes or in the Re-evaluation Counseling Communities.)

Sometimes people are puzzled at our objections to their mixing other theories and practices with Re-evaluation Counseling because they have experienced or read about other therapists performing some actions very similar to some things the Re-evaluation Counselor does with his or her clients and think that therefore the two sets of practices should be compatible.

What they do not realize, because in general they are not used to rigorous thinking in this area, is that the *assumptions* are different in the two cases, and this being so, the similarities can be ephemeral. The Re-evaluation Counselor proceeds from different assumptions and will proceed to different results than did and will the other therapist. To mix in other practices in Re-evaluation Counseling is to saddle oneself with unfaced contradictions which can lead very quickly to harmful practices which have nothing in common with Re-evaluation Counseling.

These thirty-five points characterize Re-evaluation Counseling, at least in large part. What other distinctive points about it have you noticed that I've missed?

To really care
Means to dare
To share.

LETTER TO A RESPECTED PSYCHIATRIST[3]

Dear Dr. _____ :

Thank you for your letter of June 16. My slowness in replying has been due to a summer surge of activity.

Yes, we do have a great many special techniques for facilitating discharge other than Roger's "unconditional positive regard." They are not, however, techniques of the sort that one may add to an existing structure with any hope of long-range success. The difference in the application of Re-evaluation Counseling and other approaches to therapy begins on the axiomatic level and unless the counseling proceeds from these basic assumptions, one is not likely to do much better than well-meaning therapists of any other persuasion.

One needs to remember at all levels of counseling technique that the human being is intact, complete with vast intelligence and goodness, in spite of the appearance given by the distress pattern; that the distress pattern and the human are distinct, very different entities and that completely different attitudes to each must be maintained at all times; that the counselor's helpfulness is restricted to assistance in securing discharge (with a small amount of furnishing information being the only and occasional exception); that the client is in charge of the session and the counselor is in the position of "helper," being directive only against a pattern and never against the human client; and

_RC._
Premise

---

[3] First published in 1970 as a pamphlet.

so on. These are summarized in "The Postulates of Re-evaluation Counseling" and many of the theorems derived from them are in the other published material.

Of equal importance, what makes Re-evaluation Counselors so effective in securing thorough, exhaustive discharge from their clients is that these counselors are being counseled themselves, regularly. The limiting factor for discharge for a particular client on a particular day is pretty much the free attention ("awareness," "slack," "thoughtful attention") which the counselor can turn to the client. There are many therapists who turn to their patients an "unconditional positive regard" which is so fuzzy, so rigid, and so unaware as to leave the patient still very much on his or her own, thus limiting his or her ability to start discharging and continue with it. Discharge seems to occur well and profoundly only in the company of another human and the differences in ability to discharge depend on how much that human is really present.

If a counselor is not himself or herself receiving effective counseling regularly, his or her ability to elicit and assist discharge from his or her clients will stay limited or even regress as restimulation adds to his or her own tensions. The counselor who is having counseling regularly, however, has more awareness, more slack to turn to his or her client each time they work together. The results show dramatically. Beginning men students in Re-evaluation Counseling classes, for example, frequently have difficulty in "getting" their clients to cry. Why their clients don't cry is a frustrating mystery to them. When, however, they have themselves overcome the "big boy" conditioning and discharged grief, then their clients quickly sense their openness and proceed to cry easily and well with them.

A counselor who has himself or herself been counseled successfully and profoundly frequently need only look at his or her client for that person to begin massive discharge whether in a formal or informal situation. Members of the Co-Counseling Community which has grown up around us here in Seattle frequently comment that their friends and neighbors "smell that I have some slack" and converge on them to burst into tears, tell their life story, or whatever gambit they use to begin the relationship of being counseled.

If the second person (the counselor) is not tense about discharge, then the first person (the client) will spontaneously move to it. The negative signals which the tense counselor emits are many and varied but they are received clearly, usually unawarely, by the client and his or her discharge is inhibited. On the other hand, if the counselor is not afraid (awarely or unawarely) to have his or her client cry, if he or she is not afraid to really look into his or her client's eyes, if he or she is not conditioned to not really think about his or her client, and for his or her client, then the client responds, often with dramatic speed, and begins to discharge full tilt. If the counselor is not afraid to put an arm around the client, not afraid to hold him or her in a warm, loving embrace while he or she sobs, then this will be recognized by the client who will proceed in this direction. If the counselor is acting on the basic axioms of Re-evaluation Counseling, he or she will have clearly in mind that his or her role with the client is not to analyze or understand or manipulate but simply to secure exhaustive discharge of stored up emotional or physical tension so the client can free himself or herself from the rigid patterns left by past hurts. Thus he or she is clear that when the tears or laughter stop, his or her responsibility is to redirect the client's attention to the point where the discharge can occur again and to do this repeatedly until there is no more discharge left of any sort even if this necessitates carrying on over several sessions. The client can and usually will bring up exactly what he or she needs to discharge on (even though in the case of chronic patterns, he or she brings up the opposite and depends on the counselor to guide him or her to reverse his or her phrases and attitudes so the discharge can begin).

It is the counselor who must take the responsibility for returning the client's attention again and again and again to the thought or phrase which elicits discharge because the client is simply not able to furnish this persistence himself or herself.

23

This persistence goes on past any one form of discharge. The Re-evaluation Counselor knows when the person is through shedding tears, however many hours it took to shed them over the incident or problem, that this is not the end. There is still trembling ahead if the narrative is repeated and skillful help at beginning trembling is furnished. When the trembling has taken place and comes to an end, then laughter lies ahead and then angry storming and laughter again with yawns appearing whenever the pattern of painful emotion becomes ragged and "drained" enough to permit the "core" tensions of physical hurts to disperse.

A great deal of the effectiveness of this relationship in securing and completing discharge is that it is a relationship between peers. Even the professional Re-evaluation Counselor who is being paid by the hour for his or her services regards himself or herself as "helper" of the client and feels that he or she is basically a Co-Counselor with his or her client even though his or her own counseling is being done by another person and he or she may be counseling this particular client for pay. For discharge to proceed to the profound thoroughness which it needs, it is necessary that the relationship with the therapist be a peer relationship. A "condescending savior" or "dependency" relationship is not effective, and we think it is not effective because it is not realistic.

What the client has needed all along is the warm, understanding regard of another friendly human who will not get upset by his or her distresses while he or she allows himself or herself to feel, express and discharge the stored-up upsets and be free of them. All the familiar tricks of analyzing or suggesting tend to get in the way of the client and prevent this thorough discharge and the complete re-evaluation which can follow.

Given these basic attributes of the relationship, there are many, many techniques for helping discharge to begin and persist with it thoroughly. A good counselor will tend to create new techniques within each session. These techniques do not work alone; they are effective only when functioning on these basic requirements for Re-evaluation Counseling.

With an open counselor and good rapport, the counselor often need only ask, "What do you need to say to me?" and then, with friendly insistence, "What was your first thought?" for the client to begin discharge. If the first thought is verbalized by the client without discharge, the counselor asks for quick repetition with "Again!" and yet again "Again!" Discharge usually ensues.

The "first thought" or "flash answer" question will vary, being chosen to fit the context of client and previous sessions: "What is the thought that will let you cry?" "What are you afraid to say to me?" "What's on top today?" "What do you need to talk about?" "What does Joe (Ellen) need to say to me?" Usually the counselor's quick, friendly insistence that the client actually try to voice the *first* thought is necessary. (The *first* thought will often appear out of context or unimportant to the client but it is the one that will bring discharge if followed up.)

If the counselor is well-counseled, it is a rare client who can tell the story of his or her life without spontaneously beginning to discharge. This is because the client is eager to discharge, regardless of his or her patterned appearance, and the aware attention of the counselor is a magnet for discharge. Of course, the client's voice may only break or his or her eyelids flutter spontaneously, and it is up to the counselor to focus attention sharply enough at that point (usually by repetition) for discharge to begin.

A warm direct gaze into the client's eyes is often essential. (This is *not* the tense stare or glare of the uncounseled therapist.) Holding both of the client's hands relaxedly but warmly is good communication and assists discharge (not the fishy grip or jerky clutch of the therapist who has not discharged his or her own tensions).

A Re-evaluation Counselor will hold out his or her arms for a client on the verge of tears or trembling to rush into and will hold that client as tightly and as lovingly and as long as it promotes discharge.

Setting of and coaxing and encouraging the client repeatedly to try a behavior direction that contradicts the pattern is crucial for coping with chronic patterns, and it leads to the scores of hours of heavy discharge necessary to eliminate such chronic patterns.

Deft, straight-faced mimicry of a pattern ("crowding the client out") is an irresistible weapon where the pattern prevents overt cooperation with the counselor. (Discharge is often explosive.)

All of these and an ever-growing list of hundreds more, however, only work well in the hands of an aware, growing human. His or her own success at being counseled is the Re-evaluation Counselor's basic and not-at-all secret weapon.

If I have not been clear, please let me know. I will try again. The best communication about this would be for you to see some Re-evaluation Counseling in practice, or participate in it yourself. I know your schedule must be busy, but if it is ever possible for you to participate in any of our work, you will, of course, be most welcome.

With warm regards and best wishes,

Harvey Jackins

Warm, loving humans everywhere surround us
Fogged in by fossil fears from old distress.
From out our own dissolving fogs, turn to them.
Appreciate, approve, love, touch, caress.
Their eyes and ears will struggle to come open.
Knowing themselves again, they'll grasp our word.
With tears and trembling, stormy talk and laughter,
They'll move with us to act on what they've heard.

THE COMMUNICATION OF
IMPORTANT IDEAS[4]

Human affairs are in several kinds of crisis today. These crises are not in themselves new, but are moving in these years toward some kind of climax. The existence of the Cold War has helped to make plain that rigidities in society threaten the well-being of humanity. Escalating warfare in Asia embroils the world. Nuclear armaments pose a danger to the existence of all life upon the planet. Racism, poverty, and irrational population increases are increasingly intolerable. Many people are becoming aware of these facts.

Fewer people are as yet aware of the nature or the source of the individual human aberrations underlying these social rigidities. These irrational patterns of behavior are present in every adult human; they distort and curtail every individual, group and society. Yet, because of the way these patterns function it is difficult to be aware of them.

This pamphlet is addressed to people familiar with Re-evaluation Counseling.* You *are* aware of the nature and source of individual aberrations. To you it is present knowledge that no individual need remain caught in patterns of irrational behavior. You know that only distress experiences leave irrational behavior patterns on a human being, and that thorough emotional discharge and re-evaluation will remove the sources of these patterns from any human. The alternative to remaining aberrated is an arduous alternative but a workable one.

---

[4] First published in 1964 as a pamphlet; revised in 1968.

* For a brief introduction to the concepts of Re-evaluation Counseling, see *The Human Side of Human Beings* by Harvey Jackins, Rational Island Publishers, 1965.

Many of you who have used Re-evaluation Counseling techniques have suggested that society and social problems could be grappled with rationally and need not be handled within the framework of existing rigidities. You have suggested that Re-evaluation Counseling could remove the irrationalities from individual humans who would then be free to approach social problems intelligently.

You who have seen Re-evaluation Counseling work can conceive that alternatives exist to nuclear war, that it is possible to handle existing problems and conflicts of interest in ways other than by an arms race or a "balance of terror," or by armed intervention by one country into the affairs of another. You can conceive it to be possible to apply rational methods to ending armed conflict, to the relaxation of international tension, to progressive disarmament, to solving the problems of transition to a peace economy, to meeting the real needs of the world's peoples.

(These pressing problems are moving toward solution in any case through the inevitable social processes which periodically replace societies which have become unworkable with new social structures. These blind processes, however, have in the past operated through armed conflicts and mass violence. Modern technologies make these traditional channels terribly destructive and extremely dangerous to the very existence of humankind and place great urgency on the introduction of rational, flexible behavior into the arena of social processes.)

The knowledge of how this can be done is very precious. Only parts of it are shared as yet by other groups within the population. Lack of this knowledge is what has prevented humanity from coping, so far, with the danger of escalating war, of nuclear holocaust, of international conflicts, of unworkable societies and of lost individual lives.

To communicate this knowledge effectively is a sufficient condition for solving the most grievous and threatening problems of our day. This is so since possession of this knowledge

How to Disseminate RC Awareness + Use

inevitably makes possible discussion, communication and agreement among all human beings concerned.

The effective communication of this knowledge, then, becomes a key problem. Can we clearly and effectively communicate this knowledge to all our fellow humans? If we can, how can it be done?

Let us look at the general process of mass communication of new ideas as it has occurred in the past, and then relate it to the particular new ideas with which we are concerned here.

It takes a few to challenge status quo's methods of communic.

All effective mass changes of opinion have historically come about by what has been called a social chain reaction. A new set of useful and rewarding ideas is developed by an individual or a small group. These spread throughout the population rapidly relative to the usual slow communication of new ideas or cultural attitudes. Note that these ideas spread rapidly but *begin* in the minds of an individual or small group in every case. (This is the effective answer to the discouragement patterns which say, "We are so few, what can we do?")

For a social chain reaction to take place in the past, the old established sets of ideas that governed human relations (whether their guise was religious, philosophical, political or sociological) had to become so unworkable that they were openly and obviously oppressive and dangerous to the welfare of most people. (This was necessary in the past but it need not always be so. In the future logic may replace despair as a motivator of change.)

This condition of unworkability is met by our modern situation where the future appears to be one of despair for most of the world's peoples if the ideas of the past are to continue to dominate the world.

Secondly, for a set of new ideas to spark a social chain reaction, the new ideas must bring continuous rewards to their

RC

ongoing

benefits

chain

reac.

↓

desire

for

rational

communication

possessors. Acceptance of them must bring not just momentary reward nor yet rewards only after years of adherence, but must bring reward and individual satisfaction to their possessor day after day as long as they are practiced.

The knowledge which we call Re-evaluation Counseling meets this requirement of daily reward. To understand the possibility of freeing oneself from the grip of individual aberrations and limitations, and to use the techniques for doing so, is to be rewarded continuously. This has been the experience of people who have used Re-evaluation Counseling consistently.

These useful and rewarding ideas must also include within themselves a motivation for communicating the ideas forthwith to others, once they are accepted and understood. This is the chain reaction mechanism.

The chain reaction requirement is met in that one's own enjoyment of increasing rationality, of the rewards of knowledge of Re-evaluation Counseling, is enlarged by the extent to which one has drawn family, friends and immediate environment into a similar attitude and quest for rationality. One's own rewards are limited and endangered in their larger scope by the irrationalities of society and the threatening possibility of nuclear destruction.

This is not just theory. In practice each person who has become a participant in Re-evaluation Counseling has spontaneously felt the urge to "pass the word" to others. What has not been well thought out or solved to date is the problem of communication itself. How can we transmit these useful and rewarding ideas to someone else so that s/he understands them and begins using them in his or her daily life?

There have been many suggestions. "A book on theory." (One book has been published and more are in preparation.) "Pamphlets." (There are now several, including this one.) These publications, along with lectures, speeches, television and influential supporters have not, by themselves, accomplished the kind of communication we are discussing.

There have been other kinds of successes, too. Good communication *has been achieved* many times. A substantial and growing number of people use Re-evaluation Counseling regularly and communicate its knowledge to other people at an increasing rate. Looking at these successes carefully, some key insights emerge.

The first of these is that communication is essentially a *personal, individual process*. Television, printing, tape recordings, movies, leaflets, mass meetings and lectures can only be auxiliary to and helpful with the main job of communication which necessarily takes place on an *individual, person-to-person* level.

Corollary to this is the realization that the usual avoidance of this type of communication and the rationalization that it is too slow, too tiresome, are simply covers for people's own fears and shyness which make it uncomfortable for them to attempt this person-to-person type of communication.

It is easy to demonstrate mathematically that individual chain communication, once in progress, will reach people "in time." If we start with one hundred communicators and if each of these passes the idea on to two other people within a month, decisive sections of the population will be reached within a year and a world transformation in thought will occur within two years. Not only is such individual communication rapid enough, but actually the television network one's embarrassment would substitute simply cannot do the job with such important ideas. Human beings are not built to respond in this area to anything less than another individual in person.

A second insight is why this is so. *Communication of important, new ideas can be given only to a person who likes or loves the communicator.* It is simply not possible to hear and accept anything that contradicts one's existing fears, prejudices and other rigidities as sharply as do the ideas of Re-evaluation Counseling except from a person whom we hold in affection.

Maybe

Does this impose an insuperable barrier? However much we want to communicate, most of us have spent our lives feeling very, very limited in the number of people who love or like us. It might seem that if we knew any way to get people to love or like us as much as this requirement demands, we would have already done it long ago.

Must like in order to be liked

Instead of frustration, however, this leads directly to a third insight which is something we have known for some time. For a person to love us or like us, *it is usually necessary for us to love or to like him or her*, and to communicate this to *him or her* in the first place.

What could hold us back from doing this, since the person whom we wish to love or like is that most wonderful creation in the universe, a human being? Why, only our own fears and shyness, of course (sometimes masquerading as prejudices).

Here we need not be stopped. We have at hand the tools and techniques for freeing ourselves from fears, embarrassments, shyness, self-consciousness and all similar impediments. We have a sizeable group of people working with consistent success at shedding such fears and embarrassments. The means are at hand, are available to each of us.

These means are already being used. Many of the people who come to talk to me about Re-evaluation Counseling introduce themselves with some sentence like, "John —— has been of great help to me and I'd like to learn how to be that helpful to someone else," or, "There is this woman in my office who has awareness most people don't have. I want to be that way myself, and she says counseling made the difference for her. "

Where shall we find people to communicate to? Everywhere. Everywhere around us are people as eager as ourselves for

RC alterm. to disfunc. society

this knowledge, regardless of the contrary appearances which their patterns sometimes give. All humans will wish to hear an alternative to individual unhappiness, to a poorly functioning society and to nuclear holocaust if we will communicate it so they can hear it. They will be eager to learn the tools and techniques to make this knowledge workable and the means of communicating it to others.

This is true of our families, our next-door neighbors, our colleagues and our fellow workers, the members of our house of worship and trade union and P.T.A. It is true of our classmates, our teachers and our students.

It is true of every person regardless of his or her social position or the irrational attitudes which s/he wears. It is true of the "warmonger" and of the "peacenik." It is true of the person in the White House and the person in the People's Palace of Peking. It is true of the people in the armed services and it is true of the people on whom their guns and napalm are turned.

Everywhere people are waiting eagerly, though unawarely, to be loved or liked and communicated with. When they have tried what they have heard and felt its workability, they, in their turn, will prepare to communicate it to others. Thus, all humankind will receive the missing information which it needs to solve its problems. It will receive it through the thoughtful communication of individual humans such as yourself, and, in particular, through *you*.

What to do all the time from now on:
APPRECIATE YOURSELF—*out loud, without any reservations*

> ...Appreciate yourself with appreciative, positive words
>
> ...Appreciate yourself with a proud, exultant posture
>
> ...Appreciate yourself with a pleased, happy expression on your face
>
> ...Appreciate yourself in a happy, pleased ("foolishly smug") tone of voice

Tell whoever or whatever is with you of the elegant, exquisite nature of the *real you!*

> ...Tell your Co-Counseling group
>
> ...Tell your Co-Counselor
>
> ...Tell your friend or friends
>
> ...Tell your spouse, children, and parents
>
> ...Tell the casual passerby
>
> ...Tell God
>
> ...Tell the mirror, tell the steering wheel, tell the fence post

WHY :

> You will discharge
>
> You will act rationally
>
> You will hold to a good direction
>
> You will emerge from old dependencies
>
> You will take charge of your life

THE COMPLETE APPRECIATION
OF ONESELF[5]

HISTORY

(Dianetics Orig of RC)

What we call Re-evaluation Counseling developed as a result of some accidental experiences in 1950. Full-time exploration of the phenomenon which we had stumbled upon began in late 1950, and by February of 1952 it had acquired its present organizational form as Personal Counselors, Inc.

Aree.

Spectacular successes happened often enough with these first years of "professional" counseling to overshadow any difficulties that we experienced. Dramatic changes occurred often enough and with enough clients to reinforce and increase our eager excitement at exploring this avenue that promised to answer the riddle of human warpedness and unhappiness. We learned consistently and became better and better counselors.

Yet certain distress patterns of certain clients held out against us. Many fine changes would occur with these same clients in other areas, but some distress patterns would persist in the face of all we could do. These were *chronic* distress patterns, consistently dominating the behavior and feeling of the individual, though we did not realize the distinction at the time.

Partly we were slow to realize this because, at the same time, we were having successes with other patterns just as chronic. With these, the counseling situation itself, our eager, enthusiastic

---

[5] First published in 1964 as a pamphlet.

and interested attention, the privacy of the counseling booth, etc., were sufficiently different from the contents of the pattern to achieve the necessary contradiction. Discharge would then occur consistently just as it did with the permissive kinds of counseling that were so successful with the non-chronic patterns. We noticed that these distresses required a great deal more time to discharge completely than other patterns. We spoke of them as "heavy" patterns and the non-chronic ones as "light" patterns, missing as yet the qualitative differences between them.

Student Co-Counselors had much more trouble with these chronic patterns than did the staff counselors. Difficulty in coping with one of these was often the excuse for switching Co-Counselors if not for giving up Co-Counseling.

Much discussion and experimentation went into this problem. We rigorously avoided the familiar rationalization of blaming the client for being "difficult," for "not cooperating," for "not trying hard enough," for "not wanting to get well," even though the chronic pattern often gave the client every appearance of just these things.

We began to understand the necessary factor in early 1954, and sometime in 1955 we were quite clear about the distinction between chronic and non-chronic patterns. We knew that chronic patterns are simply patterns that have been restimulated past a critical point so that they now "play all the time." We knew that clients have identified themselves with the chronic patterns and are unable with only self-generated motivation to look at them objectively. We knew that enough factors *in the counseling situation itself* must contradict the chronic distress pattern before discharge can occur, whether these factors are achieved accidentally, intuitively, or deliberately.

This was a major development. It led to much more consistent successes with every type of client. It opened the door to a much more profound estimate of the intelligence, ability, and goodness of every human, however deeply this nature is obscured by the sediments of distress.

38

CO-COUNSELING AND THE CHRONIC PATTERN

The application of these understandings to Co-Counseling has been a detailed and fruitful process.

Once the distinction in ways of handling the latent and the chronic pattern became clear, the search for dependable Co-Counseling procedures for chronic patterns began.

It soon became evident that discharge achieved from a chronic pattern tended to have more far-reaching results than the neater, tidier but also less important results of working on non-chronic patterns with permissive counseling.

With the new knowledge, discharge from a chronic pattern could be achieved beautifully on the days when the counselor was rational, aware and creative. On these occasions, the aware counselor quickly noted the direction and content of the chronic pattern, calculated an opposite direction to it and offered the phrases or actions which would put this opposite direction into effect. S/he then found the acceptable and possible avenues for motivating his or her client to use these phrases and actions to contradict the pattern and achieve discharge.

In actual Co-Counseling, however, an optimum counselor is not always available at any particular session. When the counselor was not aware, Co-Counseling that tackled chronic patterns did not tend to go well. So a search was begun for dependable directions; that is, directions which a client could take that would be "upstream" (against the pattern) under all or nearly all conditions. What was needed were directions that could be remembered or read off written notes on the days when the counselor was not "sharp."

We soon found that validation of the client by the counselor was such a dependable direction. In general, distressing experiences are not stored away which include someone being rationally validating and approving to the victim. Later it became clear that the direction of self-approval was even more dependable.

39

There are few distress experiences in which the victim is relaxedly pleased with himself or herself.

(3)

Affection

(In group meetings, it was found that the expression of affection was a dependable direction. To share and accept affection with and from a group of other humans is to contradict every hurt we ever had, apparently.)

THE DEPENDENCY PROBLEM — *counter by self-acceptance*

The direction of self-approval worked particularly well. At the same time, the persistence of a helpless, dependent attitude on the part of the client whose chronic pattern was being attacked became increasingly noticeable as a difficulty.

It was plain that the helplessness and dependency that invaded the Co-Counseling relationship once chronic patterns were attacked had its origin in the actually dependent status of the child whom the client had been at the time the foundation distresses of the pattern had been laid in. Yet the progress of the client emerging from a chronic pattern was slowed by this very dependency.

(4)

Good direction by the counselor to contradict the chronic pattern and earnest attempt to follow the direction by the client would lead to heavy discharge and a good session. At the end of the session, the client would typically tend to reverse polarity, slump into the direction of the pattern itself and stop progressing until the next session when the counselor once again would give a good direction, etc.

TURNING POINT

(5)

Unlimited self-approval

In the fall of 1963, a turning point was reached in response to the question, "How far should a person go in approving of himself or herself?" A dozen stopping points were immediately suggested by those of us discussing the question, but examination failed to uphold any validity for the proposed limits on self-approval.

LOGIC

The conjecture then followed: What would happen if a person approved of himself or herself without any reservations whatsoever? Over a period of time, this question was attacked logically, philosophically and experimentally.

Logically it turned out that any proposed limitation on how far a person might rationally go in approving of himself or herself was always rooted in a distress pattern of invalidation itself and could offer no valid stopping point.

PHILOSOPHICAL BASIS

Philosophically we began with an important distinction that had been faced early in our work, the necessary distinction between a person and a distress pattern with which the person is afflicted. It became very apparent in the very beginnings of Re-evaluation Counseling that to be effective in any human relationship, and especially in such a demanding one as that of counseling, it was necessary to sharply differentiate between the rational human and the distress patterns which have parasitized him or her.

It is true that distress patterns are attached in some way to a human and repeatedly turn him or her off and present themselves as if they were the human; but their rigid, repetitive nonsurvival activity is qualitatively and completely different from the flexible, creative behavior of the rational human. They are attached to the human only in the sense that a tick is attached to a host, or that a tin can is attached to the tail of a harassed dog.

To fail to make this distinction and on the one hand to treat the pattern as if it were the person, is to attempt to reason with it, to try to communicate with it, to seek to elicit a flexible

Pattern not logical or reasonable

Person is not the pattern.

response from it. *The pattern cannot be reasoned with, cannot be communicated with,* and is in its very nature *capable only of repetitive, rigid responses.* The person who makes such a mistake will almost certainly have his or her own frustration recordings restimulated in the process.

On the other hand, to treat the person as if s/he were the pattern is to invalidate the person, to fail to communicate, to behave as if the human were an idiot. This does not work well, either.

We had known this distinction for some time. Applying it in the context of the human's approvability, the rational human being is immediately seen to be admirable and approvable without limit. Any reservations held about the human or any canards or smirches thrown in his or her direction must really be directed at attached patterns *that are distinct from the human.*

THE EXPERIMENTAL CHECK

Experimentally it was found possible to explain the above and communicate it to a group of intelligent people.

It was found possible to secure agreement from each person in the group that this was the correct attitude to take toward each of the other members of the group. Then when the agreeing individual was confronted with a request to be logical and apply the same standard to himself/herself, to the first person singular, to face and exult in his or her own elegant nature, satisfactory discharge followed promptly.

There is a dependable direction for contradicting, discharging, and emerging from chronic patterns which can be reached by prior communication and agreement (not just offered by the counselor and accepted on faith by the client). It is to appreciate oneself in every way *without any reservations.*

unconditional

self-accep.

QUALITATIVE CHANGE

This may not seem very different from previous attempts at self-approval but the *"without any reservations,"* appearing as a quantitative enhancement of the approval, turns out to bring important qualitative improvements in the whole nature of counseling.

"Without any reservations" gives basic logical support to the direction of self-approval under any and all conditions. Any apparent "thoughts" that call for changing or limiting the direction of self-approval while engaged in trying to follow it can be arbitrarily but accurately labeled a reservation and ignored or resisted on the basis of the previous logical commitment.

HOW TO DO IT

In practice, the client is beset by reservations. The more enthusiastic the self-approval s/he attempts, the more his or her mind is invaded by the "fruit bats" of self-doubt, self-criticism, suddenly remembered and apparently genuine flaws in his or her character and the whole miserable record of his or her apparent past failures and shortcomings. These, of course, are just the recordings out of which the chronic pattern of non-survival behavior was built. To the client, however, they tend to seem more and more brilliantly logical and accurate than his or her previous logical commitment to unlimited self-approval. His or her commitment to self-approval begins to appear to be a ridiculous, mistaken fantasy which s/he has just matured away from in the last few minutes.

repeatedly

To keep the process working, however, s/he need remember only one thing, that is, to stick by his or her guns and keep expressing unlimited self-approval in words, tone of voice, posture and facial expression.

It can happen that the client will "get lost completely," that is, be unable to remember a single positive thing to say or with apparent helplessness listen to nasty negatives spill from his

Direction to go 180° fr. negativity

①

or her mouth. She or he is not without landmarks even here. She or he need only force him/herself to examine the negative thought or utterance which by then seems so sublimely logical, laboriously compute its exact opposite, the statement that would be 180 degrees in the other direction, and utter it at least three times out loud in a happy tone of voice. The negative words are thus used as a reverse direction finder. The negative statement by being happily contradicted is turned into fuel for the discharge process. Discharge is on its way once more.

STARTLING CONSEQUENCES

An important corollary of the *"without any reservations"* shift is the theoretical ending of the dependence of the client on the counselor. Once logical agreement is worked out (not to be attempted to be re-logicked in the middle of the discharge process, of course) the client is never without a direction. Always and at all times, s/he knows what to do. His or her job is to approve of him/herself out loud *"without any reservations"* in word, tone, posture and facial expression.

The distinction between direction in sessions and direction between sessions disappears. It is correct for a client in a session to approve of him/herself continuously *"without any reservations"* utilizing to the fullest the attention of his or her group or counselor. At the end of the session and until the next session it is just as correct for the client to approve of him/herself *"without any reservations"* to friend, fellow worker, family, shaving mirror, steering wheel or fence post.

At the beginning of his or her next session, it becomes correct for him/her to approve of him/herself "without any reservations" to his or her counselor or group, etc. The client never has to wait for someone besides him/herself to tell him/her what to do. Many sessions in the future will undoubtedly have the counselor begin by asking, with this implied agreement on direction already established, "And what do you need to do today?" For the rest of the session, the direction will be left up to the client.

COUNSELOR CHANGES, TOO

We have enough experience already to make it plain that the counselor who is used to giving directions has a re-training period ahead of him/her in which s/he learns to wait for the client to give his or her own directions. No matter how slow the process may seem to be at first, when the client does take the steering wheel in his or her own hands without external urging, the resulting discharge will very rapidly make up for any slowness in the beginning.

The counselor is not left idle or passive in giving up his or her old directive role. There are an infinity of ways to assist the client in his or her appreciation of him/herself and the counselor is much more effective as s/he "assists" in this way, than s/he was "directing" in the more elementary kind of counseling.

GROUP MEETINGS WITHOUT DEPENDENCY

Group meetings flourish especially well this way. The giving of directions, which used to seem so necessary, was inevitably an invitation to restimulation, tangle, and group difficulties, since good intentions were no safeguard at all against directions being given from patterns instead of from rational awareness.

Now we can dispense with directions completely, once the group meeting itself begins. The available time is divided evenly among those present so that each person has so many minutes to have the rest of the group pay her/him full, friendly, aware attention as s/he appreciates her/himself. The other people are free to discharge also during her/his turn but they have agreed to pay attention and to make no "helpful" suggestions. The order of turns can be assigned by drawing straws or any similar procedure.

If a member "forgets" and "wastes" her/his turn at one meeting or even at several meetings, that is strictly her/his business. The others will refrain from scolding or "helping" her/him. When s/he does get around to using her/his turn well, it will be under her/his own power and will have much greater results than if s/he is "helped."

A person having a turn before the group may ask and be given any assistance s/he desires from another member or from the whole group except being told what to do or what to say. This is her/ his sacred right and duty to figure out for her/himself.

It seems to work well for there to be a short discussion before the group session itself begins, for the members to refresh themselves on their direction and the use they intend to make of their time before the group. These discussions can well be a statement, by each group member, of what s/he understands about appreciating her/himself. These discussions will often be creative. At the foggiest they can consist of reading the contents of the box on page 36 of this book. The discussions seem necessary to refresh the "appreciate oneself" direction against the only difficulty it encounters—the difficulty in remembering it and remembering to do it.

BREAKTHROUGH

There are many indications that the "Complete Appreciation of Oneself" is very close to the ultimate direction for emergence from all irrationality. Every time it is applied, it works. We seem able to better remember to do it the more we practice it.

Consistent practice of it by many people is the next step.

Up from inanimate, out of one-celledness,
Gaining complexity, structure and plan,
Changing, evolving at last to intelligence,
Maturing, we make it to Woman or Man.

The struggle, repeating each fresh
                              generation,
Exposes each one to distresses and pain.
When healing is blocked then illusions
                              anachronate
Delude us that past situations remain.

Large, we feel little. When safe, we feel
                              threatened.
Informed, we plead ignorance. Free, we
                              hear chains.
Powered, we act helpless. We cling to
                              dependency.
While ours gather dust, we trust someone
                              else' brains.

Idiot societies bully and threaten us,
Herd us through ruts of disaster and blah,
Inflaming our scars to secure our conformity,
Blindness perpetuate, unreason raw.

Once only heroes dared rise up occasionally.
Now, all who read this know how to discharge.
Who guides <u>your</u> steering wheel ? Powerhouse?
                              Universe ?
If it's not you, then just WHO IS IN CHARGE?

WHO'S IN CHARGE?[6]

Each of us who has attempted to use Re-evaluation Counseling for his or her own progress has come up against certain interfering attitudes of his or her own. These attitudes become attached to us as part of the distress recordings which we all bear. These recordings are different each one from the other, since each arose from a unique experience, slightly different from any other distress experience. Nevertheless, certain similarities usually tend to occur in any given culture because many aberration patterns have become chronic in the culture and are a part of our cultural conditioning. Thus they are enforced in a similar way upon all of us.

One of these common types of patterns is what might be called the "helpless" pattern. The content, spoken and acted out repeatedly, is that one has difficulty because of something outside of oneself. We feel, act, and assert that some other person or circumstance, apart from ourselves and our patterns, is stopping us from acting or achieving as we wish to. This kind of pattern is carried in some form by all of us, though in a rare individual it will be so contradicted and submerged by compulsive responsibility patterns as to seem lacking to casual observation.

One source of these patterns is imitation of the similar patterns which our elders wear, since these elders are the source of a great deal of our information. If we accept these models during distress, uncritically, they become combined into our distress patterns, and we dramatize helplessness later in manners and phrases which the patterns of our elders used.

---

[6] First published in 1964 as a pamphlet.

*Dependency
as Child* A second source is that the foundation incidents of our patterns of rigid behavior occur when we are children, when in actual fact we are quite dependent and unable to take full responsibility for ourselves. Not only are we weak and without information, but also we are often enforced into helpless roles. At the time the earlier distress recordings are made, there is an element of dependence, of being unable to be in charge of things.

Daily, for each of us, the rational need to act responsibly comes into conflict with old feelings of helplessness. Daily, we succumb to the feelings and fail an opportunity; or, less often, we resist by calling upon other distress feelings to resist the helpless ones, for example, "working up a mad" to help ourselves do the things we are afraid to do.

One sometimes blindly makes a decision that it is better to *try* than to despair. Such desperate reasoning has served in many crises for many people.

Actually, the reality is more reassuring than that.

All of us who are adults are in fact *always* able to be responsible. If we look closely at the *realities* of our lives, it can be demonstrated for each of us that we are able to take charge and have our lives go the way we want them to.

All of us have the capacity to manage our lives because all of us have a very large amount of intelligence at our disposal if we can remove the distresses that inhibit it so that it can function. With the knowledge of Re-evaluation Counseling which all of you reading this possess (or can possess), you have the possibility of doing just this.

Each human being, each one of us, is in full charge of the entire universe. This is a strong statement but it is logically meaningful.

The universe—as far as our relation with it goes—actually is our universe, and it must necessarily be centered on each of us.

We are not here setting up a subjective structure or pretense and turning away from the reality of the universe that exists. To face the realness of the universe of which we are a part is the first step in taking full charge.

We assume the reality of the objective universe. We *cannot prove* its existence. Philosophers have previously demonstrated this with complete logic. The reality or non-reality of the universe is an axiomatic question. We can assume that it is real or we can assume that it is a projected idea. We must assume one or the other if we wish to deal with the universal impression that there is a universe surrounding us.

The idealist philosopher chooses to assume that the universe is a mental image, a figment of someone's mind—God's mind, a human's, the philosopher's. The realist philosopher assumes that the objective universe exists independently of whether humans think about it or not.

In practice, both philosophers act on the realist's assumption. The idealist philosopher behaves like the realist when s/he goes down to breakfast in the morning and eats her/his ham and eggs just as if they were real.

We choose the realist assumption, of course. We assume that the objective universe is real for the very down-to-earth reason that this attitude leads in practice to more interesting and useful results, and because it is aesthetically more satisfying.

We assume that the universe is real, that it exists quite independently of human thought about it. But when we come to dealing with this universe, to human manipulation and improvement of it, we are not able to come to grips directly with this reality. We can only take in the sensory impressions reaching us from this real environmental universe, and from these construct a mental model of the universe as we know it.

Individual may create useful model of world

Each of us must necessarily construct her/his own unique model. No two of us can receive identical data or hold identical viewpoints. In practice it turns out that the more direct one's sensory contact and the more self-reliantly one builds one's model (i.e., with the least uncritical borrowing of others' conclusions), the more useful the model becomes.

These separate models which we build can be brought to any desired degree of agreement by communication and improved perception. Actually, conflicting viewpoints do not persist except where aberrations inhibit the thinking process.

Yet each of these models will necessarily contain the viewpoint of the model builder, and this viewpoint must necessarily be unique. Thus the models cannot be identical in any absolute sense.

(If the distinction between "agreement to any desired degree" and "not identical" seems confusing, let us resort to an analogy from mathematics. The rational fraction $1/3$ can be written in decimal notation as .33. This is very close to $1/3$ but it is $33/100$ which is not exactly $1/3$. However, no matter how small a difference we specify for our decimal number to vary from $1/3$, we can achieve this accuracy. We can do it by writing .3333 or .33333 or as many places of 3's as we wish or have the time or paper to write. Thus we can produce a decimal number which is less different from $1/3$ than any specified difference, but we cannot represent $1/3$ decimally in any absolute sense—no matter how many 3's we write.)

This unique mental model which we construct is, then, the universe that we are in charge of. No one else *can* be in charge of it. This is *our* model. It is a more and more accurate description of what the objective universe is, but never identical with it, always including the viewpoint of the model builder.

Changes in the real universe will occur as a result of the activities which we have initiated acting on our model. But these changes will be reflected by changes in the models of all of us if we remain aware, perceptive and rational in this logical way. Each of us is necessarily in charge of this universe of ours—all the universe there can be for any one of us—to manipulate, to master, to improve and to enjoy.

The universe which we can apprehend, grasp, manipulate and enjoy spreads out from us individually in every direction. It is the nature of the human being at its center to be intelligent, to take charge. No other creature that we have knowledge of possesses this ability.

Perhaps some day we will meet some other such creatures in a visiting delegation from some distant planet or star. Until we do, a human being is the most complex and the only largely rational creature that we have knowledge of. We simply *are* the best there is. Only *we* have the capacity for manipulating the environment and managing its progress.

The principal obstacle to our fulfilling this role thoroughly, to our all-around enjoyment and satisfaction, is exactly the distress recordings which drag behind us like unwelcome parasites and which tend to discourage us or inhibit us from assuming this active responsibility for all things.

To resist these patterns is a necessary step for intelligent functioning. When we talk of full responsibility for the entire universe, we are in the first place trying to get a realistic picture of the role assigned to us by our nature. We also seek, however, to set up safeguards against the insidious effects of irresponsibility patterns.

Responsibility

If we compromise with the patterns of feeling inadequate to any extent, we will accept a limit to our responsibility. We will rationalize, perhaps in familiar phrases: "How in the world could I be held responsible for that?" Or, "There must be a limit to what a person can be responsible for . . . ."

Actually, no; there is no limit. We must take full responsibility, each of us, for the farthest atom of the farthest star in the farthest galaxy, because if we set any limit to our responsibility, then we have logically abandoned all responsibility. We have opened ourselves to the impact of the irresponsibility patterns. A reactive lack of principle will have been established so that soon we will be excusing irresponsibility on things very close to us in our environment.

There is an old Norwegian folktale about the good man who, with his old wife's approval, decided to take their precious second cow to market and exchange it for something even more useful to them. As the story unwinds, the good man (an "impulse barterer") exchanges the cow for a less valuable horse, the horse for a sheep, the sheep for a goat, the goat for a pig, the pig for a rooster and, as hunger pangs develop, the rooster for a sandwich, which he consumes. The valuable cow had been quickly transformed into no property at all, and once the first impulse trade had been accepted, each step that followed was quite consistent. The actual point of the folktale was quite positive. The old man recoups his losses magnificently by betting his neighbor a hundred dollars that the good wife will approve of everything he has done, which she proceeds to do, beaming approval for her husband's wisdom in each trade he recounts, and thus winning the hundred dollars for him. The step-by-step loss of the cow, however, is analogous to the erosion of our responsibility—once we accept any limits on it.

Responsibility or irresponsibility is one of the "yes-no" questions in our lives, like an "on" and "off" switch on a light. The light is either on or off—it is not a little bit "on." There are many questions which are gradual in our behavior. We can be tall or taller; we can push against an object with infinite variation in our pushing force. But we are either completely responsible or logically not at all, and our patterns deceive us when they attempt to set limits to our responsibility.

To say that we are responsible for the entire universe does not mean that we have at any present moment the capacity or resources to do everything that we might wish with all these parts of the universe for which we are responsible.

Certainly we must look at our resources, our capacity at any given moment, and assign these resources rationally to the things in the universe which concern us most. It may be that our present capacity toward the farthest atom mentioned above is simply to be aware of it; but it is important that we *be* aware of it and not shut it out of our mind as if it were of no interest.

Certainly we must put our attention and resources on our own lives most, next toward the lives of our immediate families, next for the lives of our associates and members of our interest groups, our city, state and nation, next for all humankind; then for other forms of life, the physical world, etc.

This is for the *assignment of resources*. It is not for us to be responsible for ourselves *first* (in a time sense) and *postpone* responsibility for our family. Actually, we must be responsible for all at once for anything workable to happen. We will put in more time and attention on our own job. Most important, we must see that our own job goes well. We will rationally assign time and attention to our immediate families to a much greater extent than we will our bowling team or our hobby club. Yet we must take full responsibility with whatever resources we can allot on *all* levels or we will be in trouble on all levels.

It is familiar behavior the world over for the frightened citizen's fear recordings to say: "I am not interested in politics; I must look out for myself." When grave issues confront the nation (such as the rise of fascism in the 'thirties, or civil rights and the threat of war today), recordings say: "Leave that up to the big shots . . . ," "You can't fight City Hall . . . ," "I'm going to look out for myself . . . ."

It's easier to see that this sort of attitude does not work if we choose examples a little away from us. Let us consider the German citizen who, when Hitler's recordings were corrupting the German nation, excused her/himself from resisting or for going along with Hitler's program by saying that it wasn't her/his concern. This rationalization allowed her/him use of the loot from the robbed peoples of Europe; it helped her/him rationalize her/his feelings of guilt at the persecution of the progressives and Jews. Very immediately, it did *not* protect her/ him from the death of her/his son at Stalingrad, or her/his own death under mass bombings.

A fearful Japanese citizen of Hiroshima might easily rationalize that s/he could not resist the Emperor or the War Cabinet of Japan, and that it wasn't her/his responsibility to do so. Her/his fear and helplessness recordings might tell her/him that s/he could only look after her/his own little job and her/his own immediate family. Because s/he did nothing effective in the years when the Japanese war machine was building, because s/he accepted limits to her/his rationality, because s/he did not take responsibility, s/he and her/his family died in the glare of the atomic bomb.

These examples are easy to see. They are no more illustrative than similar behavior in the United States, in Seattle, at the present time.

We must be in full charge at all times. We will allocate our resources of time, capital, attention, ability, as rationally as we can. We will not accept limits to our responsibility or our concern.

To assign the responsibility for any difficulty to an external factor, or to another person, or to another person's recordings, is itself a recorded irrationality. This irrationality "feels" reasonable

Blame

since all of us have become conditioned to doing this. To blame, to reproach, to say that the cause of the difficulty is elsewhere, is as useless and destructive as self-reproach or guilt. Someone else's pattern may have initiated a difficulty, or we may be rationalizing and be unaware of our own patterns' tense behavior which triggered the reaction over there. It makes no difference "who started it." If we stick on ". . . It's not up to our conventions," we tie our hands in terms of solving the situation.

It's something like the old safety campaign posters: "S/he had the right-of-way, but s/he's just as dead as if s/he had been wrong." It doesn't really matter in terms of solving a situation whose "fault" it is or was; in fact, "fault" and "blame" turn out to be nonsense concepts having no useful meaning. The real question is always: "What can be done to solve the problem?" The first thing that can be done always is that the initiative to work things out can be taken by the first person singular. If we stand around and point the finger of blame or say: "I can't act because of this or because of that . . . ," we have tied up our own tremendous ability to solve problems and make things go right. We have allowed the recording to rehearse its dependency message, its impossibility message, its hopeless message. When we defy the recordings and take charge of the situation, then something can be done. Someone has to take charge for our successes to occur. *We* have to take charge.

CC Specifically in a Co-Counseling situation, Co-Counselors can become tangled in mutual restimulation. To blame each other or to blame oneself is then the most useless thing in the world. The questions with meaning are always: "What can I do to correct the situation?" "What counseling theories and techniques can I use to untangle this snarl?" Once this attitude is adopted, things begin to happen.

There is only one person in charge of your universe. Some rationalizations offer God as an excuse for being irresponsible. They say that God is really in charge, not "little old helpless me."

You will have little difficulty with this. If God is in charge of the universe, S/He has certainly placed *you* as a working superintendent of the you-centered universe with which *you* deal and is not likely to excuse you from your job.

Cold logic? No! For logic knows to care
And care effectively. It's fear that's cold,
Illogic cringe short-sighted, selfish, failing;
Nor is there warmth in sympathy to share.
That's just the throbbing of distresses old
In tune with ours, agreement with our wailing.
Only the zesty, eager human mind
Will always notice, care, and move to action
For self, for loved ones, and for all Humankind.
Warm logic brings success and satisfaction.

THE LOGIC OF BEING COMPLETELY LOGICAL[7]

The Addiction Phenomenon and Its Remedy

RC purpose

In our progress toward more complete mastery of the environment, we who use Re-evaluation Counseling frequently notice confusion arising from acting on the basis of "feelings."

In other discussions we have carefully separated "feelings" into "natural feelings" and "feelings of distress." In theory we assume that the natural feeling of a human being is zestful enjoyment of living and that all distress feelings are the result either of distress experiences immediately present or of past distress experiences which have been stored as recorded patterns and which have been re-triggered by present events.

In actually distinguishing between rational and distressed *behavior*, however, the label of "good" and "bad" feelings has turned out to be an undependable criterion. Certain distress feelings are subjectively described by their victims as "good" or even "delightful" because such an assertion is part of the distress pattern itself and is apparently verbally concurred in by the human victim when the distress pattern is operating.

---

[7] First published in 1965 as a pamphlet.

FLEXIBLE VERSUS RIGID

The reliable criterion for distinguishing rational from reactive behavior turns out to be the question of its rigidity or flexibility. The response is rational if it is new, accurate and workable in the particular situation. It is recorded and irrational if it is old, repetitive and ineffective. One cannot determine the rationality of a particular attitude or response by whether the person making it reports feeling "good" or "bad."

I recall a client once reporting: "I was awfully uncomfortable, but I stayed aware this time and I handled things differently. The people looked surprised but they seemed to like it. Things worked out fine!" Here was a report of "uncomfortable" feelings, but a rational response.

On the other hand, there are many narratives like these: "That whiskey was too good to pass up. It was a wonderful spree, but I surely have a mess on my hands now!" "I'm no hero; I gave up quick once the pressure was on, and I didn't accomplish a thing. It was just too uncomfortable the other way. . . . "

VERY SIMPLE ANIMALS, VERY RIGID RESPONSES

There is some reason to think that simple animals (arthropods and simpler) are immune to what we think of as pleasure or pain, i.e., they are lacking in any *general* responses of the kind that we associate with experiences we term "pleasant" or "unpleasant." Creatures on this level seem to have very specific responses triggered by very specific agencies—the flavors of certain foods, the specific attractant odors of members of the opposite sex, the "food discovery dances" of other members of the hive, and so on. "Pleasant" and "unpleasant" (as general concepts) seem to have little meaning in discussing the behavior of insects, crustaceans and the like. An early naturalist reported feeding a dragonfly its own abdomen which, presented in this way as food, it ate with apparently good appetite.

MORE COMPLEX ANIMALS, PLEASURE-PAIN CHOICE

Mammals and birds certainly have a more generalized kind of response, a discrimination which has been called the pain-pleasure decision or the pleasant-unpleasant choice. With birds and mammals other than human beings, this mechanism seems to have some survival value. To avoid pain or a too unfamiliar environment and to seek food, sex, companionship and familiar surroundings is a notch above the clockwork behavior of the grasshopper or the hermit crab. This operation of choosing a response based on whether pleasant or unpleasant feelings are aroused is easy to observe in mammals other than humans. Trainers of animals use this response to condition the animal, that is, to warp or distort its inherent responses into new forms more useful to its human masters.

Because this mechanism is easily observed it has been used as a basis for explaining animal behavior and animal "learning," so-called. It has been used over and over again in attempts to explain human behavior. These attempts have succeeded in explaining almost everything about the human being except her/his humanness.

FOR DISTRESSED HUMANS, REGRESSION

The potentiality of the "seeking of pleasure-avoiding of pain" type of behavior persists in humans in some kind of latent anachronism even though humans have evolved to a rational capacity. It persists because a human being meeting distress subsides for the duration of the distress to a more primitive level of functioning. Her/his rational intelligence, her/his ability to create new, precise, accurate responses, suspends.

While unthinking, s/he tends to respond on the more primitive basis of avoiding the unpleasant and seeking the pleasant, of retreating from discomfort and grasping at any kind of "comfort." These acts then become recorded as part of the distress recording and are in the future likely to be repeated by the individual whenever s/he is restimulated and compelled to re-enact the recorded experience pattern once more.

FEELINGS NOT A RATIONAL GUIDE

People's first experiences with Re-evaluation Counseling often lead to a great improvement in their "feelings." They feel uncomfortable while they are discharging but once the discharge is at an end and the session is over, they often feel light-hearted and free. Understandably, in the absence of adequate theoretical guidelines, these new clients or Co-Counselors tend to think of the "good" feelings they are now enjoying as the goal of their counseling. In a session they are still somewhat willing to feel their old distresses while they discharge them but they expect "good" feelings after a session and between sessions. They may try to choose a direction for their own progress on the basis of whether such a direction leads quickly to "feeling good" or not.

This misses the point, the real point, of Re-evaluation Counseling, which is its role as an avenue for the re-emergence of human beings to complete rationality. Once the rational ability was evolved or created in a human being, this ability to think flexibly, to come up with a brand-new accurate answer based on one's own goals is the only acceptable guide for a human being's behavior. *Feelings* are not at all a dependable guide to action in a rational human sense.

For a human, feelings are to be *felt, not acted upon.* "Good feelings" can be enjoyed but they are no substitute for thinking. If the urgings of our feelings coincide with the direction of our logical thinking, fine, so much the better, but it is still our logical thinking that is our guide. If our logical thinking goes counter to our feelings, then the more our actions contradict our feelings the more we will feel them (and discharge them) but our logically-thought-out direction will be the direction we try to follow, not any direction our "feelings" urge upon us.

People have recognized this intuitively. When one's child is asleep in a burning house, the feelings of fear and pain urgently direct one not to enter the fire which will hurt her/him and threaten her/his life. Instead, the human being feels the pain, faces the risk and rescues the child, and human beings everywhere applaud it as the human thing to do.

The same sort of issue is met less dramatically many times a day by each of us. It is met in its clearest form when we attempt to use Re-evaluation Counseling.

ACT CONTRARY TO FEELINGS

A person, for example, after discussion and agreement, sets a direction of always appreciating her/himself without any reservations. S/he knows ahead of time from her/his counseling experience that s/he will feel like a fool as s/he does it. S/he knows it will *seem* irrational to do it once the old feelings of invalidation begin to throb and before they discharge. Yet s/he continues to appreciate her/himself in spite of the feelings.

As s/he continues, discharge will occur repeatedly, often without her/his noticing it. Profound changes occur, not only in her/his daily behavior but also in her/his fundamental outlook. S/he becomes a more totally rational person, in greater mastery of her/his environment.

True, when we discuss this direction as a policy in a group of Co-Counselors, we are likely to hear loud outcries, groans and other indications of discomfort. "Be logical all the time? Ugh!" "You can't do that all the time, a person just needs to flop and relax once in awhile." These are not responsible contributions to the discussion. These are only expressions of the familiar discomforts of going against an aberration pattern, of moving upstream, of being responsible. This kind of discomfort is a good discomfort. It is a satisfying discomfort. It is the satisfying discomfort of discharge, the discomfort of sticking to a diet and losing weight when one craves to be gluttonous, the discomfort of keeping the house picked up and fit to live in, the discomfort of having been patient with a child who needed our patience even when we had a headache.

THE ADDICTION MECHANISM

The other kind of discomfort is the kind that masquerades as "comfort" or "need." It is the "numbness" of being swamped in a hurt pattern. It is the "comfortable" feeling of being shut down, of being stupid in a familiar way.

The heroin addict swears with perfect sincerity that it feels "good" to get a shot of heroin, that it is a wonderful experience worth all the waste of her/his life and others. Heroin is a poison that hurts the human deeply when injected. This hurt creates a distress recording which acts to compel its own repetition, just as any other distress recording does.

The confirmed alcoholic is apparently sincere in her/his recorded insistence that getting full of alcohol is the only desirable way to live. Alcohol is a sedative that shuts down the rational ability and installs a recording of the experience of being full of alcohol. This recording acts to compel its own re-playing, getting the human full of alcohol again, just like any other distress recording.

This is what addiction is: the insistent urge, usually rationalized and defended, of a distress recording to take over the human, shut down her/his intelligence and replay itself with the shutdown person acting as its puppet. We are addicted to being fearful, to introspection, to yelling at our children, to blaming others for our difficulties, to blaming ourselves for everything. We are addicted to whatever is the content of our hurt recordings.

MANY ADDICTIONS ARE INHIBITING

Not all addictive urges are active ones, to be logically contradicted by refraining from action. Probably the majority of chronic distress patterns are inhibiting in character, passive in their effect, apathetic in their tone.

These patterns urge their victims to stay in bed, to put off decisions that need to be made, to not take responsibility, to refrain from initiative, to follow rather than lead, to accept a subordinate role. They insist on things being "easy," i.e., not contradicting their chronic feelings.

COUNTER WITH RESPONSIBLE INITIATIVE

To act logically for any person requires assuming full responsibility, seizing and keeping the initiative at all times, playing an active, leading role, and accepting that the rewards of a rational effort are usually proportional to the difficulty of that effort.

New humans, i.e., unhurt babies, are continuously active and aggressive when not asleep, are ceaselessly and happily probing the environment and extending their understanding and control of it. This is still our real nature when we are adults, beneath the concealing patterns of distress. Our logical behavior will be active in accordance with this nature.

Acting on logic alone offers a workable tool for smoking out, identifying and resisting these addictive urges. Allowing feelings to be included as a guide to action leaves us helpless to tell a goal from an addiction.

MANY ADDICTIVE PATTERNS

"The good taste of whiskey" says the ad and the addict repeats the words. Ask an unaddicted child what whiskey tastes like.

"The clean, fresh taste of a He-Man Cigarette" says the television commercial and the conditioned addict. What does it taste like when someone else blows their cigarette smoke in your face?

"I need to think this thing through" rationalizes the introspecting pattern as it retires its captive human away from the decision s/he needs to face and make. How much thinking is done as the human introverts and shuts down?

AGAINST THE FEELINGS, LOGICALLY AND HIGH-TONED

Recovery   The dependable direction for emerging from all irrational patterns and regaining full humanness is that of acting on logic *at all times*. Holding this direction, we do what needs to be done even though we feel afraid. We resist restimulated feelings of grief and depression while we get the chores done. We try to force a smile, not only to spare those around us restimulation by our droopy expression, but also to contradict the restimulated grief. *If we contradict it enough,* tears will flow in full discharge and we will emerge from depression *permanently.*

Many people have in the past tried to urge a similar direction upon others. There are hundreds of cults and self-improvement systems and books which urge one to "think positively," "boost, don't knock," "turn the frown upside down." Some people have been encouraged and helped by these exhortations while others have been bewildered.

For this kind of direction to become effective, a full understanding of discharge and of a Co-Counseling relationship is required. With these as a foundation, it becomes fully effective.

CULTURAL RIGIDITIES

Not only feelings viewed as negative by our culture must be excluded as guides to action. Feelings which our culture will often label as praiseworthy must also be resisted. We may feel tremendous "sympathy" for someone, but if we act on it without thought, without awareness, we can easily find ourselves in the familiar situation of waiting on a "helpless" chronic pattern, of feeding a "sympathy seeking" aberration and being of great disservice to its victim in so doing.

LOGICAL ALWAYS

All human beings need to follow their own logic in *all* their actions *all* the time. Those fortunate human beings who have with awareness grasped the tools of Re-evaluation Counseling have a special opportunity and responsibility to progress toward uninterrupted functioning on this basis. Feelings will be felt, but need not ever be used as guides to action. If our "feelings" happen to concur with our logic, fine. If they happen to oppose it and we act on our logic, then we will certainly feel our feelings but we will just as certainly discharge them and be free of them, without letting them guide us in the process.

The ways of our society
Are not all as we'd have them be.

A new society could be
A new kind of rigidity.

Only distresses made us hate
And fear and not co-operate,

And, since each human rigid grew,
Society grew rigid, too.

As we emerge from old distress
To individual happiness

There's time to think about the key
To taming our society.

THE FLEXIBLE HUMAN IN
THE RIGID SOCIETY[8]

Thoughtful people express concern that the pressure for conformity presently being placed upon young intellectuals will
dampen or prevent the emergence of the thoughtful innovations
necessary for the self-renewal of society.

Sometimes discussions appearing in learned journals try to
resolve the conflict the authors feel between anti-social behavior
and the need for innovation by treating the problem as if it were
one of degree, as if a little non-conformity is good but that too
much is bad and dangerous.

The insights which our theory of human behavior afford us
make it possible for us to say confidently that the difference is
of kind, not degree. They also make it possible to see that this
is not a problem of young intellectuals alone but is a manifesta-
tion of a general difficulty with which every human contends.
The human's essential nature is one of flexibility, but all present
and past societies, even though they have been constructed by
humans, are essentially rigid.

How do we account for this?

---

[8] First published in 1964 as a pamphlet.

WHERE WE BEGIN

In the viewpoint from which I speak, the viewpoint of Re-evaluation Counseling, every human being is an essentially rational creature. We assume that a human being functioning on his or her inherent nature comes up with new, flexible, workable responses to each new situation which s/he confronts. S/he computes correctly when s/he has sufficient information; s/he actively seeks additional information to improve his or her accuracy. We are quite sure that the human being is inherently happy, zestful, loving and cooperative with other humans.

The unhappiness, irrationality, failures, and conflicting activities associated with humans as we know them are assumed to be acquired characteristics. These are residual effects of distress experiences which the human has suffered. These are effects which s/he has not succeeded in throwing off because the healing mechanisms which are available to him/her for recovery have not functioned. These recovery processes (characterized outwardly by tears, trembling, laughter, etc.) have not functioned because of conditioned social behavior which has compulsively interfered, continually and insistently, with the operation of these mechanisms.

THE ORIGIN AND DEVELOPMENT OF SOCIETY

Social organization inevitably must have emerged simply because of its survival value. Any manipulation and mastery of the environment past the most primitive level becomes easier with cooperation. (Two heads are better than one; four hands are better than two; many hands make light work; you scratch my back and I'll scratch yours; etc., etc.). The cooperation involved in care of the young has been with us since our evolution as mammals. The family group heightens the survival value of its members when it becomes a clan, and so for the clan when the clan becomes a tribe. Given the frightened, largely irrational humans that our early ancestors must have been, progress in human mastery of the environment would have been very difficult in any other way except through social cooperation.

Once established, however, a human society made up of partly irrational individuals had inevitably to become a super-organism with a life and continuity quite distinct from that of the individual lives of its members. The analogy has often been made of the individual humans comprising society in the way that the individual cells of the human body comprise the human. The analogy is valuable to the point that society is at least as different a type of organism from the individual human as the individual human is a different type of organism from his or her individual cells.

The organism of *society* has its own laws of existence and development, quite distinct from the laws for individual humans. This is a necessary result of its different character, of its different composition and organization.

Social rigidities must have become established as a necessary condition for dealing with the individual rigidity, the result of the individual distress patterns. These distress patterns are the results of individual distress experiences. The social rigidities are developed to counter, suppress and limit the problems arising for society out of individual irrationality.

THE PRACTICAL APPLICATION

A significant number of people in contact with each other have embarked on a consistent attempt to evade this conditioning social pressure, which interferes with their use of their mechanisms of recovery. They seek to revive and use fully these mechanisms of recovery. They seek to regain to the fullest possible degree the use of their inherent, rational abilities, their cooperative functioning, and their capacity for enjoyment. They assume, and by now have pretty well demonstrated, that they still possess these capacities once the inhibiting distress residues are removed.

The work which we call Re-evaluation Counseling is the rediscovery and application of means to accomplish these goals.

SUCCESS BRINGS A NEW PROBLEM

People moving very far in the direction of more rational behavior find themselves confronting certain aspects of the society in which they live which they have previously accepted and submitted to but which increasingly seem to them to be irrational and anti-survival. Serious practical conflicts occur and must be faced and solved. When these are discussed with others who are moving in the same direction, the whole role of society, of social rigidity, of social structures and customs, tends to be called in question. Over and over again, and in many forms, people ask the question: How can a rational human function in this society of today?

This question has been raised and discussed from other viewpoints many times. It will be in process of being answered from this viewpoint for a long time to come. We can usefully speculate in a limited way at present.

ANALOGOUS TO ORGANIC EVOLUTION

Society's operation resembles in many ways that of a non-thinking organism such as a sponge or coral colony. The colony operates as a whole even though it is made up of large numbers of individual creatures. Society operates on rigid patterns of behavior similar to those of pre-human organisms. It evolves *new* rigid patterns of behavior only by a kind of evolutionary process analogous to the evolution by mutation and natural selection of pre-human organisms. More effective societies tend to conquer, destroy or absorb the less effective societies with which they compete for land, food, prestige, or markets.

A primitive cooperative society based on primitive production methods and on the scarcity of wealth that flows from them inevitably gives way internally or externally to a slaveowner-slave society. This happens when improved production makes enforced cooperation by the slave a more effective source of wealth than the production motivated by hunger and whim of the primitive cooperators. The slaveowner-slave society is supplanted in its turn by the more effective baron-serf society. The baron-serf society is overthrown, internally or externally, by the capitalist-wage earner mutation of the social organism.

For the working out of this spontaneous, unplanned kind of evolution, we have the agencies of political and economic conquest, we have wars, and we have revolutions. These agencies, vastly destructive of the human beings comprising the societies, have never destroyed *all* of the competing societies themselves (up to now) but have been agencies for the emergence of better organized and more powerful social structures which have at least the potential for better survival for their individual human members.

AN UNPLANNED PROCESS

These blindly arising evolutionary changes in society have in the past functioned almost independently of individual human intelligence. In each particular case, they have always succeeded against the opposition of large numbers of individuals who fought to oppose change and to preserve the old order.

Typically, individual rationality has assisted or expedited these blind social evolutions, unaware of its own role and motivated by other considerations than the social changes it served. Individual intelligence has here served these social changes largely through creating political, religious, or social theories which have rationalized or expedited the spontaneous changes. We may think here of early Christianity as assisting the downfall of the Roman slave society, of Luther nailing his theses to the door at Wittenberg in unaware behalf of the rising merchant princes of Germany, of Commodore Perry forcing the ports of Japan open to world trade. There are many others.

Social functioning and social change have, until now, been almost entirely unguided by individual rational thinking, and they have severely circumscribed such rational thinking. The intelligent advertising man of today, for example, does not plan effective ads to induce people to smoke more cigarettes and thus bring lung cancer upon themselves because his individual welfare or that of his fellow men is served in any intelligent way. He does it because of a blind mechanism of his society called the market which requires that people be induced to smoke cigarettes so that tobacco can be grown, processed, transported and sold for the wages and profits which participants in the tobacco industries feel helpless to obtain in any other way.

DESTRUCTIVE CONTROLS

Society's controls over its individual members, being rigid, have been destructive in their effects upon the individual. Enforcement of individuals has never enhanced the broad rational survival of the individuals enforced. Neither has enforcement been very good for the individuals enforcing (though we might have to have a separate discussion to clarify and establish that point thoroughly). Punishment has never been effective in producing pro-survival behavior among humans, not once in the thousands of years of its repeated application. Wars have always been openly destructive of the individual humans involved, though only at this hydrogen bomb point has the complete destruction of society itself become a possibility. Yet enforcement, punishment and war have continued and continue in spite of their obvious irrationality from the standpoint of individual human intelligence. They have continued because the *rigidities* of the social organism have required them.

The conflict between human intelligence and social rigidity has, till now, been quite one-sided. Any individual who has persisted in an intelligent attitude in conflict with a social rigidity has always been labeled *"officially unintelligent"* (and subversive) and has been punished, forced into line or destroyed. The martyrs were thrown to the lions or crucified; Socrates was served hemlock; Billy Mitchell was forced out of the service; the Mississippi Freedom Workers were murdered and bulldozed over.

The individuals who have pitted their individual intelligences against social rigidities and have triumphed, surviving individually or at least in glorious posthumous legend, have been those whose efforts coincided closely enough with evolutionary upheavals and the mutation of society to a new form. Their intelligence served at that moment the blind needs of social change and was protected and honored by the new social creature it had served.

Society has been something like a great unthinking creature, even though its individual members have been human beings who sometimes think.

CAN INTELLIGENCE TAKE CHARGE?

Is it possible at the present time that human intelligence can at long last deal successfully with social irrationality? The record of the past would seem to be one thousand percent against this possibility; but there are some new factors present and growing that in my judgment indicate precisely this is now on the agenda for humankind.

One of these factors is that society has already evolved through many stages and has, stage by stage, changed to permit increasingly larger numbers of its individual members to become informed and responsible. Hardly any slaves had access to much knowledge, few serfs could read or write, but almost all American wage workers are literate, and modern industry pays wages to thousands of engineers and PhDs.

Second, the technical progress which is almost the sole positive result of any society has now brought excellent communication facilities which carry with them the possibility of communication between large numbers of the individual humans who comprise society. (Television networks can not only sell cigarettes and beer, but they can also present such a position and person as that of Mrs. Fannie Lou Hamer of the Mississippi Freedom delegation at the Democratic National Convention of 1964.

Telstar may very well actually communicate to large numbers of people, previously unreachable and afraid, that all humans are indeed one family.)

Third, for the very first time the survival of society itself is threatened by irrationality rather than, as up to now, the survival of individual members only. If very many hydrogen bombs go off in the old irrational way before rational procedures supersede, then it will be not just part of the human race but most or all of it that will be destroyed, and society itself will be destroyed in the process.

Finally, a special reason. Most clearly from the viewpoint of Re-evaluation Counseling, but to a considerable degree from many other viewpoints arising today in the world, the fundamental distinction between rational and irrational individual human behavior is finally being faced and procedures are being worked out for converting one to the other.

Can flexible human intelligence attain control and ride herd on this great irrational creature called Human Society? Can we make it perform to our intelligent collective will in a way analogous to the performance of the domesticated horse, dog or elephant? I have indicated that I think we *can* and, in fact, are on the historical verge of doing so.

SURVIVAL IN THE MEANTIME

Another question of even more immediate interest to each of us is whether it is possible for an intelligent individual to cope with the rigid society before it has been domesticated and tamed. Next week, next month, next year . . . can rational people who are in the process of becoming more rational find a workable way to live well among the rigidities of the society of which they are a part?

This issue has been posed in various forms by many thinking people. Present-day intellectual discussions often concern damage caused by social pressure for "conformity."

Many of the young people who intuitively resist the rigid pressures to conform become caught in rigid rebellions instead. Avoiding conforming to Madison Avenue by becoming a dropout ends in another kind of conforming and is not a happy result.

NARROW CHOICE UNNECESSARY

Is it necessary to choose between conforming to the rigidities of society and succumbing to one's own rigidities? Can we perhaps avoid or resist the enforcements of society without relying on the rigidities of our own individual painful emotion, without becoming prey to our own resentments, fears and despairs?

Can we "stand up to" society? Can we afford *not* to when society speaks for social rigidity? Do we have to resist unintelligently when we do resist? Are there other alternatives besides rigid conformity or rigid rebellion?

I think we can say with complete confidence, yes, there are other alternatives. The individual rational human *can* survive well and flexibly even within the existing rigidities of society. The more rational and flexible s/he becomes, the better s/he will survive. The requirement for good survival in this rigid society is precisely rational thinking as we define rational thinking, that is, the calculation of brand new, exactly accurate responses to all new situations.

How can we plan to survive well?

FACE CLEARLY

First of all, let us face the fact that the rigid society *does* exist. It will not go away simply because we cry out at its blindness or unfairness. That we discover its irrational nature and protest loudly against it has little or no effect upon its behavior or operation. Millions of people before us—almost every human in fact—have so discovered and so protested without the structure or operation of the society being altered to any appreciable degree. Protest often preceded and accompanied change, but change actually occurred only when society itself was ready to evolve to a new form. Let us face that society exists as it does—rigid and irrational—and when it changes it can only change to a new kind of irrationality (as in past changes) or, possibly, in a new kind of change become subservient to human intelligence.

Society will change, not when we feel outraged, but only when internal pressures require change or when human intelligence moves flexibly in a new way to accept control of society and to domesticate it. Irrational society is a fact at present, an important fact, and one of many facts which a flexible intelligence will not ignore, but will include in its evaluation of each situation.

NOT WITH SUBMISSION

A rigid society is not the sole fact in any situation. It is not an *overwhelming* fact. It does not need to *dictate* our responses. Rigid society is not an absolute truth, not a God-given permanent difficulty to prostrate ourselves before or adjust ourselves to.

Much social conditioning presents society to us in this way and cements and conditions this attitude by punishment. The rebels of the past who have defied a ruling monarch or other particular organ of society have suffered repression. They have been called traitors to God and Duty, betrayers of Faith, Honor and Patriotism. The free-thinker who would *unskillfully* call in question the strictures of his or her own society had best have a hide-out in the hills prepared.

Yet, having faced without distress the rigidity of society as a *fact*, then that fact deserves no different kind of treatment from the human intelligence than any other fact. Society deserves simply to be evaluated and understood for exactly what it is: a blind irrational creature not yet evolved to the intelligent behavior of its most rational members. It is *not* an all-powerful despot.

We need to face the reality of irrational society. We need to avoid accepting either surrender to its enforcement or irrational rebellion against it. We also need to adopt as our own long-range goal the *conversion* of society to intelligent behavior, i.e., taming it to be subservient to the intelligence of the individual humans who comprise it.

Society cannot require conformity. It can only require the *appearance of conformity.*

FIND OTHER ALTERNATIVES

We need to use our own intelligence to foresee possible conflicts with the rigidities of society and to plan alternatives to either conforming or rebelling in a rigid way. *It is always possible to do so.*

It may be possible to steer clear of the conflicts completely. If your beloved residence is in the path of a freeway, you might get busy politically and acquire some influence toward re-routing the freeway. You might raise your sights and find yourself an even more charming and beloved residence and make the occasion one for moving up in the world. You do not have to choose between submitting unhappily to eviction or standing to defy the bulldozers with a shotgun.

A mad bull elephant may seem determined to charge down a particular path on which we stand. Yet we do not have to choose between panicky flight or sturdy defiance while being trampled. It is possible to turn the elephant's charge in another direction or watch the charge from a safe tree, enjoying the unusual sight.

REACH THE HUMAN BEHIND THE RIGIDITY

We need keep always in mind that the rigidities of society are carried out by individual human beings who are necessarily caught in individual distress patterns themselves in order to be able to act in such an irrational manner. We need remember further that even though caught in such a pattern, there is a flexible, rational human being behind each such distress pattern—a human who will rejoice to be able to be flexible and act in a rational manner if helped to do so. A smile and a friendly approach have interrupted the writing of more than one traffic ticket.

The techniques of Re-evaluation Counseling present more profound tools for reaching this flexible human consistently and for assisting her/him to be free to cooperate with you. When you reach the person whose distress pattern is acting as the agent for a social rigidity, you will circumvent any damage from the social rigidity.

We need to master the distinction between the human being and the parasitic pattern. We need to master the distinctly separate skills of dealing with human and of dealing with pattern.

SHED OWN RIGIDITIES

Each of us needs to protect and extend his or her own rationality. This, of course, is the central purpose of Re-evaluation Counseling.

Doing this requires in part that we face clearly the distinction between acting *logically* and acting *on feelings*. (This distinction needs a separate and extended discussion.) Making this distinction allows us to commit ourselves whole-heartedly to the logical course and will bring the discharge of old distress feelings when such feelings are consistently contradicted by logical behavior.

Accepting and facing total responsibility for our entire environment is a necessary part of acting fully rational, as is farsightedness and a long-range point of view.

In practice we will find we need to establish rational communication and cooperative relations with other humans who share or can be encouraged to share these viewpoints with us.

NO WITHDRAWAL

To withdraw from participation in the society of which we are a part is not an effective way of survival. If we attempt to resist playing a role in the concerns of being a citizen, if we attempt to resist participating in the processes of government, to not vote, to not campaign, to not run for office, to avoid jury duty, to refuse to join organizations, we will, of course, still be playing a role, but the most irrational role of all. We will be abandoning the attempt to exert rational influence within the rigid structures of our society. We will function as puppets made helpless by our own fears. We will become ants in the social anthill. The full irrationality of society in its presently extremely dangerous form will have free sway to operate against our individual survival.

The rational individual *will* participate in the social processes. One needs to operate as fully as possible at all levels of the social organism.

SURVIVAL, SUCCESS AND ENJOYMENT

The increasingly rational human can not only survive amid the rigidities of today's society but can do so zestfully and victoriously. S/he can survive well, on the highest level. S/he can operate in rigid society much as a hummingbird can fly flexible figure eights and double loops around a clumsily flying crow or vulture.

The rational human need not be a martyr to draw people's attention to the need for social rationality. If this ever was needed to be done, it was extremely and completely done a long time ago.

The *example* of splendid survival and enjoyment is the needed communication for humans today. As the rational band of successful people grows in numbers, it will grow by recruiting to its ranks the liberated prisoners of the rigid society who no longer conform through fear nor rebel through resentment or despair.

Rational individuals will live an increasingly good life as they help other individuals take the road to rationality. They will guide society to evolve to the domesticated instrument of the rational humankind it was intended to serve.

HUMAN LIBERATION[9]

Oppression and exploitation take many forms in our society. A powerful, technically advanced nation oppresses and exploits weaker nations. One economic class oppresses and exploits another. An ethnic majority oppresses and exploits the ethnic minorities. Men oppress and exploit women. Adults oppress and sometimes exploit children.

These conditioned social processes impose many hurts upon the victims of oppression. Deep distress recordings are installed and repeatedly restimulated and reinforced in the oppressed people, recordings which tend in the direction of submission, self-invalidation, hopelessness or, occasionally, of blind resentment and ineffective resistance. The oppressors, too, are hurt by acting so contrary to their human natures and become full of recorded guilt and shame and fear of those whom they oppress.

In fact, the persistence of oppression is dependent on the installation and continual reinforcement of these distress recordings. Economic and power considerations are obvious motivations for exploitation, but we have had enough clear glimpses of what humans are really like to know that no human could continue to play the role of oppressor or exploiter unless distress recordings were making her/him numb and unaware.

The social rigidity of oppression is enforced *blindly* upon the members of an oppressive society. Resistance to oppression also arises as a *blind* social force. Struggles to end oppression in the

---

[9] Appeared in *Present Time* No. 11, April 1973.

past have largely been conflicts between two blind social forces, with only occasionally the intervention of intelligence.

The final end of social oppression will be dependent on ending the domination of humans by distress patterns. In this sense Co-Counseling is a profoundly basic, ultimate process. The re-emergence from distress patterns which we Co-Counsel to achieve is the dependably long-range channel for achieving the liberation of humans from all oppression.

I do not think that it is the only channel, however, or that it can work alone. It seems to me that those Co-Counselors who sincerely urge that our program for social change be limited to individual Co-Counseling are being influenced by fears, misinformation and indoctrinated apathy, of which they are usually not yet aware, which an oppressive society has imposed on them against any challenge of its domination.

I think our emerging intelligences must find ways to challenge and halt the baleful, continuing effects of social oppression by direct social action as well as individual re-emergence. We need to be in close contact with all movements for human liberation, helping them shed their rigidities and become effective while we serve as models of intelligent social struggle ourselves.

At the same time, we must look to our own discharge and re-evaluation and place these tools in the hands of all those who struggle for human liberation.

To neglect either front, it seems to me, is to cripple our effectiveness against patterns and against social oppression. A two-pronged attack—direct, intelligent struggle for social change on the one hand and persistent, effective Co-Counseling on the other—will make the total struggle effective and our own freedom a continuing attainment, not postponed to some distant realization of social liberation.

CHilDREN NEED POLICY[10]

A correct attitude by a parent to a young person does not include permissiveness to a pattern that is creating difficulties for the young person (and the people around him or her).

A young person being forced by a pattern to be messy, destructive, or thoughtless of others needs a firm interruption of the pattern by the parent (or other aware adult). The interruption will usually bring discharge and then, of course, the discharge must be permitted and assisted thoroughly.

To not interrupt such a pattern is to abandon the young person to behavior which spoils his or her relationships with others and prevents much of his or her enjoyment of the world.

---

[10] Appeared in *Present Time* No. 9, October 1972.

O Parents, Teachers, and all such Instructors,
Permit them learn.
                            Each mind is thirsty-eager.
If never blamed, nor scolded, nor negated;
No single "No!" nor "Wrong!" to leave confusion;
No disapproving frown to mar affection;
Each grows more thirsty and more eager always.

A little at one time is knowledge's portion
And that related to things known already.
No more until the last has been digested,
Related, understood, communicated
Back in the learner's words to the instructor.
Without this nothing justifies proceeding.

Once understood, new portion offered swiftly
Lest boredom's tarnish dull the mind's quicksilver.
Banish all tests, all grades, all kinds of ratings.
These only rate environment and teacher,
And much-confuse the learner about learning.

Love openly and well the eager learners
And twice as much the ones whose hurts prevent
    them.
Loved and approved, they'll find ways to discharge.
Then let them weep and shake and laugh and temper
And treasure the keenness of the minds emerging.

THE NATURE OF THE
LEARNING PROCESS[11]

It is possible at the present time (1966) to outline the main features of the learning process in human beings and locate the main obstacles to learning in the usual teaching or learning situations. Some immediate remedies can be proposed and long-range ones outlined.

ASSUMPTIONS

This discussion will not re-summarize basic theory in any detail. This is now available in other publications. It will suffice to say that we assume that human intelligence consists of an ability to respond to each new environmental situation with a new precise response, formulated from the similarities and differences of the present situation to and from past experiences, and an ability to file the new information from the present event in a form usable for evaluating and responding to future events.

Unintelligent behavior is the failure to respond intelligently. Unintelligence is responding with a not-new, *rigid*, pattern-from-the-past which is more or less inaccurate in meeting the present event.

Unintelligent behavior takes place when (a) the individual is undergoing physical or emotional distress or (b) when s/he is experiencing the "replaying" of the recorded residues of past

---

[11] First published in 1966 as a pamphlet.

89

physical or emotional distress experiences. These recorded residues are triggered into activity by similarities of the present events to the past distressing ones.

Intelligent behavior and unintelligent behavior in humans are regarded as completely distinct from each other. At a given time a greater or lesser share of a human's total performance may be under the influence of each of the two kinds of behavior, but the two kinds of behavior do not shade into each other. There is not a gradual spectrum of unintelligent to intelligent behavior. Each kind of behavior is "on or off," "yes or no" in its effects, although each may be dominating only a portion of the human's total performance at any time.

It is assumed (and this is supported by all observations to date) that intelligent behavior or intelligence is the natural, inherent nature of a human being. Unintelligent behavior, although it appears to parasite upon (or attach itself to) certain primitive mechanisms latent in the physical make up of the human, is unnatural and uninherent. Unintelligent behavior is always acquired and moreover acquired *only* through experiences of physical or emotional distress. The unintelligent behavior effects of distress experiences are retained *only* when such experiences are not followed by complete release of tension and by re-evaluation.

(The release of tension is accomplished in specific processes, undoubtedly very complex, but dependably characterized by the outward indications of *crying with tears, trembling with perspiration, laughter, angry noises with violent movements, yawning, and lively talking*. We describe all of these processes with the term *"discharge."* All of these tend to occur spontaneously in all interpersonal relationships, but are severely inhibited by cultural conditioning against them—the "don't cry" enforcement, for example. The practice of Re-evaluation Counseling consists essentially in allowing, encouraging, and assisting these discharge processes to operate completely, exhaustively and profoundly. Re-evaluation, the rational mental process which follows thorough discharge, does so spontaneously once discharge is complete.)

LEARNING IS NATURAL

Careful observation confirms that it is fundamentally natural, easy and pleasant for a human being to learn new things. This built-in eagerness to learn exists in all humans, though it is obscured in many. It may be explained in many ways but it certainly exists. A human being functioning in a human manner is continuously eager for new information, new insights, new experiences, new skills. Permitting this inherent attitude to operate is the key job in the promotion of learning.

LEARNING IS NOT CONDITIONING

Learning consists of evaluating new information in relation to information that we have previously understood. What has been called "rote" learning or "conditioned-response" learning or "remembering-it-long-enough-to-pass-the-test" learning is not learning at all in the meaning of our definition. This type of rigid-response conditioning is not desirable or useful in a human sense. The human is capable under certain severe pressures of doing a great deal of this kind of rote absorption but it is not really useful to anyone. The pressure for this kind of rigid response which dominates so much of our present educational procedures is damaging to the students involved and, at best, useless to society.

FACTORS WHICH PREVENT LEARNING

If learning is to be done intelligently, it follows that the learner must be able to be intelligent. S/he must be functioning in an intelligent, human manner if intelligent learning is to take place. This means that the learner must *not* be distressed, either by new distress or restimulated distress. A human being cannot learn in the real sense of the word if s/he is hurting, is overtired, depressed, frightened, embarrassed, ashamed, angry, confused or bored. A learner must be *feeling good* in order to really learn.

This is not an easy requirement to place before a parent or educator, but it is a minimal one. In home, classroom, factory, or office the learner must be *feeling good* and *feeling good about her/himself* for the learning process to have a chance.

If pupils are unhappy or uncomfortable, they can't read; or, if they are pressured into rote reading, they will not understand what they have read.

MAKING LEARNING POSSIBLE

Before teachers or parents attempt to communicate information, they need to be sure that their pupils are relaxed and feeling good. There is no use expecting to communicate information well until the pupils are in a relaxed, aware, eager attitude.

This may seem like an enormous job to classroom teachers. Many of their pupils arrive in class already conditioned to shut down and stop thinking just by the classroom situation itself. Many arrive still under the clouds of some upset from home, from play, from a previous class or from what happened in the halls. Nevertheless, re-awakening must first be accomplished or learning will not go well. Otherwise teachers will go through the forms of education without accomplishing useful learning.

In spite of the pressure of time, more will get done if time is first spent in arousing the students to a happy, receptive mood. Learning will then go rapidly. The terrible destructive pounding on locked minds which exhausts and discourages pupils and teachers alike in so many classrooms will be avoided.

REMOVING THE BLOCKS

How can this be done? By the use of the discharge and re-evaluation process to whatever degree is necessary. Severely distressed students will require much time and assistance to emerge to the level of easy learners. They cannot become good learners without this, however, and they can become good learners if they are given it. A classroom teacher will not be able to easily handle the most deeply distressed students in the classroom situation, nor be able to quickly bring them up to the level of the least distressed in learning ability. These need special attention and classes with similar students where, at first, all the class time can be devoted to untangling their distresses enough for them to learn. There are increasing tendencies in school systems to make some kind of separation of the "slow learners" but, except where the intuitive wisdom of some unusual teacher has operated, there has been little progress in converting the "slow learners" to fast learners. The separation is not enough. The problems must be *solved* as well.

Even in a classroom situation, however, and with the small amount of time that can be taken, a great deal can be done by the teacher to awaken and alert the intelligence of the students and make it available for the learning process.

The gifted teacher does many of these things intuitively. With the situation and the theory understood clearly, however, all teachers can begin to be much more effective, at least up to the point where their own distresses interfere.

BEING LIKED

Students need to know that they are loved or liked by the instructor. The relaxed teacher who has had a warm, secure childhood communicates this with a look or a tone of voice. The rest of us may have to enunciate clearly through clenched jaw muscles, "I like you, John; it is good to have you in my class," but we can at least do that and the student will respond out of all proportion to our effort.

APPROVAL

The learner needs to feel accepted and secure in the learning situation. The teacher who remembers to say, "The whole class did well on this last chapter and I'm proud of you all" will rub off some warmth on the ones who till then felt that they didn't understand the chapter at all. They will then be able to pay better attention to the next chapter.

FEELING OF SUCCEEDING

Learners need to feel that they are doing well. They always are, but this requires basic philosophical clarification for many teachers to understand. The point is that the learners are always doing the very best they can if one takes into account (which is the only realistic thing to do) all the tensions and pressures which drag upon them. If they are all doing the very best that they can do, then they are doing very well. If the teacher sincerely communicates to them that they are doing very well, this in itself relaxes the grip of the tensions upon them and automatically leads to their doing better.

Skillful teachers have known for a long time that students learn better when they are given lots of encouragement and praise. What we are saying here is *why* this is so and *how* it can be put into effect. Even the teachers whose own childhoods were long ordeals of fault-finding, reproach and discouragement can, with this knowledge, interrupt the fault-finding noises they have a tendency to make. They can deliberately heap praise on their students and begin to unhook them to learn freely.

NO MEANING WITHOUT CONTEXT

New information can be understood by learners only if they can relate it to information which they have *already* understood. To try to force them to "learn" an item of information without it being related to familiar information is to create a distressing experience for the students. They will be bored at the very least and quite likely frustrated, anxious or even despairing.

This is basic: *human beings cannot intelligently take in information that they cannot relate to what they already know.*

Under pressure, they may make some desperate emergency connection such as, "This is like those other bewildering things that I have been told I'd better remember if I want to pass the test." Some frightened children actually operate on this sort of tenuous connection to the degree that they get all A's in school and even receive their PhD's at the appointed time. Because the information has never been related well to anything except getting good grades and passing tests, the holder of this kind of a doctorate is able to do only routine work and cannot be a creative member of a research team.

If students are aware and alert on a particular day, they will need fewer reference points furnished by the teacher or communicator to evaluate new information to what they already know. They will remember a number of references from the past and will make additional reference points of their own. They will learn more easily and better even on their good days, however, if the teacher points out the relation of the new information to some already known material.

SUCCESS BRINGS ALERTNESS

Students who are only partially aware and alert in the situations provided for learning will tend to become more aware and alert if the new information offered them is connected with furnished references to what they already know. This is so because the evaluation process is itself a rational operation. To be able to grasp and understand new information will arouse them, will pull their attention away from the distresses that were clutching at them and bring them up to an alert learning level. What the person in the instructing or teaching role can do is to offer such reference points and ask the learners for others if he or she wishes the learning process to function well.

A mother once told me that her small son had repeatedly asked her what a lumber yard was when they passed one on a streetcar ride. She said that she had answered him, "That's a lumber yard, son" many times on successive trips, but that he never failed to ask again just as if he had received no answer at all. She said that, finally, on one such trip when she heard the familiar, "What's that, Mom?" accompanied by the pointing finger, she suddenly realized that he had been given no answer *in any useful sense*, and this time replied, "Well, you know how people build houses out of boards, don't you? Like they nailed the boards together to make that house across the street?" And when he said, yes, he knew about that, she then said, "Well, that place is what we call a lumber yard. It's the place we keep the boards until we need them to build houses." At which point he said, "Oh!" in a tone of deep satisfaction, and never questioned her again on later trips.

CONTEXT MUST COME FIRST

If the first attempt of the teacher or parent to offer references from the new information to the learner's present knowledge does not succeed, then the effort must be made to find other reference points. The learning cannot take place until these points are found. It is worse than useless to offer the same statements over and over again (often in a louder and louder voice). We see how useless and harmful this is when we see the tourist shouting louder and louder in his efforts to make the "ignorant foreigner" understand U.S. words. We will be appalled when we first face how much of this is turned on our children without it ever being noticed.

GOOD REPETITION NECESSARY

Though senseless repetition is of no use or worse, thoughtful repetition of information is almost always necessary for good communication. Any communication will tend to become confused, distorted, or misunderstood during the process of communicating. The confusion which enters the message and garbles it is called "noise" or "static" by communication theorists. It arises from all the interfering factors, actual noise or static, other mechanical factors which distort the signal, but in particular, from the reactive recordings which beset both the communicator and the listener. Repetition of the message several times will tend to eliminate the usual mechanical distortions, and thoughtful, varying repetition will help get around even the reactive recordings. To communicate more than once means to attempt to speak more precisely using better chosen words in a clearer tone of voice. It also means to offer a succession of new sets of reference points for the new information.

THE LEARNER MUST TALK

Learners must have an opportunity to think about the new information. In order to think very well about it in the conditions in which all humans find themselves today (inhibited by distress patterns), they must usually have a chance to communicate about it to someone else. This could be in a letter, in an essay, or in a silent prayer, but the easiest and most effective way is for them to talk about it.

This is why someone doing a good job of communicating information must stop at short intervals and ask for information back from the learners. The learners can then talk about the new information and expedite the relating of it to what they already know.

A specific question should be pointed in this direction: "What other animals does the armadillo remind you of? Have you ever heard of armadillos before?" Reports and recitations accomplish some of this in the usual classroom procedure, but because they are tied to the oppressive and discouraging phenomena of grades and "work," they accomplish their good only incidentally. This is why the "each one teach one" procedure is such an effective learning measure for the very easy learners (and can be helpful to the "slow learners"). The teaching student in attempting to communicate to the learning student is powerfully assisted in the evaluation and the actual learning of the information himself or herself by the chance to talk about it to someone else. There's an old saying that "you don't really understand something until you can teach it to someone else" that bears on this point.

When the learner talks about the new information, the teacher must firmly resist criticising, correcting or finding fault with what the learner is saying. The words "no" and "wrong!"

should be exiled from the teacher's vocabulary. The teacher can wait until the learner is through talking and then re-state the information correctly. But "pointing out where he or she is wrong" or "correcting" the learner will only interfere severely with the learning.

A LITTLE AT A TIME

The information must be presented in small increments for evaluation to take place. Too large a package of information is as bad as none at all simply because the evaluation process is jammed by the frustration of not being able to make references fast enough to keep up with the material.

The development of teaching machines (though not living up to the sweeping hopes of their sponsors) did focus attention on this necessity for small increments. The programming of the machine forced the developers to be aware of the problem's existence. It was then easily seen to be a problem in all the older types of instruction as well. Any learner needs to learn just one small thing at a time in order to really learn it. Anxiety and haste for speed in instruction on the part of teachers (and often on the part of students) frustrates the learning process and often insures that little is learned through tackling too large increments of new information. A great deal could be learned in the same time if the information were divided into small, well-organized, step-like amounts. One cannot "learn to play the violin" as a unit task, but one can learn how to finger one note and then how to bow that same note and then do the same for other notes, scales, exercises and sonatas.

LEARNING ITSELF MOTIVE ENOUGH

The only issue which should be before the learner should be to learn and to understand the information. To pass a test, to get a good grade, to be promoted, to avoid ridicule, to escape punishment, to please parent or teacher, to compete with one's fellows; these are all poor motivations compared to the basic, often-unused one—*the built-in desire to learn.*

Almost all tests, examinations, grades, warning slips, and even honors, interfere profoundly with the ability of students to learn. The way these institutions now operate it is possible for learners to feel good about themselves only if they achieve a perfect test score or the highest possible grade. To receive less is to be officially stamped "wanting, defective" to some extent. This instills anxiety recordings which will consistently and chronically interfere with the ability of learners to learn.

NOTHING BUT SUCCESSES

A good learning situation should make it impossible for the learner to make a mistake. Disappointment is instilled and confidence is weakened whenever a mistake occurs, and further learning then becomes more difficult. Dr. Frank Laubach's dictum that "no teacher should ever ask any questions to which a student can possibly give a wrong answer" arose out of the practical necessity of being effective in mass literacy campaigns. The principle is equally valid in all learning situations but the dead weight of reactive tradition obscures it in most of our classrooms. When the right question is asked the right way in a learning situation, the student will give the right answer. This should be the occasion for congratulations and approval, for the enjoyment of success by both the learner and the instructor. This in turn will make each of them more alert and make further learning go even better.

IMPOSSIBLE TO OVERDO APPROVAL

When introducing these procedures into a learning situation that has been handled badly for a long time, great emphasis and time can be taken for congratulations and approval. The instructor need not worry if the class temporarily drops a chapter behind in the text. Once their eyes are bright and their minds are working again from the approval, recognition and encouragement, they can wade through the lesson material much more rapidly than ever before and this time really learn it.

TOUCH TO TEACH

Touch can play a useful role in helping to convert an unlearning situation to one in which learning can take place. The student who is not learning is tense. Loneliness is an ingredient of almost all tension and one of the surest ways of contradicting this is to actually be in physical contact with another person. With primary grades, effective teachers have often resorted intuitively to taking children on their laps in order to introduce them to the learning process. An arm across the shoulders, a squeeze of the arm or a hug, all given with warmth and friendliness, can immediately penetrate barriers that thousands of words will not touch at all. "Get in touch" is an excellent suggestion relevant to the person to whom you wish to communicate.

TREMENDOUS ACCELERATION POSSIBLE

Finally, it needs to be said that the learning process can and will accelerate if some of the right things begin to be done and the wrong ones interrupted. A good deal of the time and effort of most learning situations is wasted in dull repetition, in rote drills, in tests, grades and so on. As learning begins to proceed well, it will acquire a strength of its own and brush over many of the old obstacles like a stream cutting through a mud dam. It should easily be possible, for example, for children to learn all the mathematics ordinarily given to them in the first eight years of school (including the new math) in a year or less, to learn it well, to understand it and remember it and to retain it in a useful form forever.

THE PLEASURE OF LEARNING

A class such as this will be a great pleasure to both students and teacher. When communication is operating well in a classroom, tests and grades will be unnecessary. The teacher will simply ask the question, "Does everybody understand everything about the axioms of the real number system?" and if the students reply, "Yes," then that particular topic of study is completed. Under present rigidities it may still be necessary for the teacher to put an "A" on each student's report card or, if the particular rules do not permit all A's, to have the students draw their own grades out of a hat, understanding very well that they are only cooperating with an archaic rigidity until it can be gotten rid of.

Learning, approached sensibly, fully utilizing just the things we already know about it, will become again the joyful process that it was for all of us in the beginning.

Afoot or horseback, rocketing or rowing,
It helps to give some thought to where
we're going.

THE NECESSITY OF
LONG-RANGE GOALS[12]

One delightful aspect of reality is that the future can never be predicted precisely, that it will always contain surprises. Our fears have longed for complete predictability, but this is only our fears. Boredom is a far worse fate than terror, and boredom would be our lot if the future were completely predictable.

This ultimate unpredictability of future reality is not due just to our lack of knowledge. Even if we could ever attain complete information about present reality, the future would go on being surprising.

SUITED TO OUR NATURES

This fits our essential nature well. We evolved in our dynamic universe, and we represent a sophisticated, highly-developed aspect of its dynamism. Our fears and hurt patterns may long for stasis, but our real human nature likes to swim in strong currents, harness moving forces, likes to feel challenged by fresh complexities.

We meet the challenging, on-rushing future with flexible, rational human intelligence. We calculate and re-calculate continually what the *probable* nature of future reality will be and plan accordingly. Only this type of flexible forecasting enables us to stay in charge of the environment and take advantage of the surprises as they appear.

---

[12] First published in 1972 as a pamphlet.

AN ADDITIONAL TASK

For all of us (so far) an auxiliary chore must be faced and handled. None of our intelligences are as yet free from the inhibiting, interfering effects of distress patterns which past experiences of hurt have left upon us. We must struggle against the effects of these upon our intelligence, and struggle to free our intelligence from them, *at the same time* that our intelligence is having to cope with reality and anticipate the on-rushing future.

It is as though zestful, enthusiastic swimmers joyfully mastering the current of the exciting stream must also at the same time compensate for the effects of, and try to free themselves from, concrete boots which were cast about their feet during past periods of helplessness.

In doing these jobs well, an aware, thought-out system of goals is very helpful.

THINKING ABOUT THINKING WHILE THINKING

Another nice thing about the reality of being a human being is our ability to be aware (and even to be aware of being aware).

I can't specify exactly what awareness for a human being is. In a logical scheme I would have to call it one of the undefined terms. (You either know what I mean when I say "awareness" or you don't.) However, people usually have some sense of the difference between being aware and not being aware. Nearly everyone cherishes experiences of being unusually aware, of being pulled to awareness by the thrill of a beautiful morning, of a new experience, or of clear communication and understanding with another person.

Awareness is not the same as rational intelligence, because a great deal of rational thinking (defined as the creating of a new, accurate response to each new experience) takes place below awareness. We use the aware levels of our rational thinking for high priority questions only. We tend to shut down on these levels if interesting, demanding, new-information situations are not forthcoming with some regularity.

Perhaps awareness consists, at least in part, of being able to view and think about the processes of rational thinking while these processes are taking place. In this way awareness or aware thinking would be analogous to a meta-system, a framework larger than rational thinking in which rational thinking is embedded and from whose larger viewpoint we can understand and decide questions which would be un-understandable and un-decidable if we were to stay within the confines of rational thinking itself.

THE PAST BECOMES INFORMATION

We expend a great deal of effort in our Co-Counseling to free our attention from involvement with distress recordings of the past and to allow it to function in "present time." Yet when we are functioning free of restimulated involvement with distresses of the past, we naturally and intuitively take the past into account in our understanding of the present and project our desires and anticipations onto the mental screen of the future. We take many *present* actions with the aim of helping our projected *future* hopes to come about.

Similarly, a good part of our progress in our own counseling is to "find ourselves" as individuals, distinct from the pressures and identifications which society and distresses have foisted upon us. We discharge and re-evaluate to free ourselves from the "shoulds" and "have to's," to think *for* ourselves, *from* ourselves, and *of* ourselves as trustworthy and sovereign individuals.

INDEPENDENCE BECOMES COMMUNITY

Yet when we attain a measure of such independent intelligence, when we have been able to think of ourselves as individuals distinct from all others with our own goals and purposes, then we spontaneously tend to also think of ourselves as a group with other human beings. We become able to link our survival potential, mentally, with that of our families, our groups, our species, and our environment and universe in a meaningful way, free from identifications and distress.

A TANGLED BEGINNING

In a sense, all those who seek to discharge and re-evaluate themselves free from their distress patterns are starting out in the middle of a great tangle of patterns with not much perspective on their positions or where they are going. The extreme difficulty of this position has been somewhat mitigated as the years have gone by, by the accumulating experiences of others. Beginners at the process of discharge and re-evaluation can now be guided to a considerable extent by what other people have done. This is the role of Re-evaluation Counseling theory, to summarize these experiences of others to afford perspective for oneself.

Even so, in the beginning of Co-Counseling it is as if one is trying to fight one's way out of a surrounding tangle. One is not sure in which direction to go. Fortunately it has turned out that any anti-pattern activity tends to bring discharge. Though the discharge may be random for some time, it affords occasional glimpses of the real nature of people and their real relations to the world. These glimpses expedite progress and allow the beginning of purposeful directions.

With a direction, one's counseling progresses. Even though random discharge of painful emotion should eventually and theoretically get rid of all the accumulated distress which people carry, the enormous amount of hurt experiences which they have lived through makes random progress a slow business in practice. It is much more profitable and efficient to discharge material with some direction rather than do it blindly. Thus, very early in one's progress toward rationality, one begins spontaneously to set goals, to plan on definite achievements through counseling.

THE BEST KIND OF LIFE

Socrates said, "The unexamined life is not worth living." From my own esteem for life I would stop far short of such a harsh judgment. To me it is a tremendous boon to be alive at all, and to be alive and intelligent is one of the luckiest occurrences that could ever befall. To be alive for only a moment, even though it were in agony, is infinitely preferable to never having been alive at all.

Yet Socrates was trying to emphasize something important. To live in the best way, to really be intelligent in the highest sense, is to be aware of what is going on, to take charge of the situation, to have ideas of what kind of future we want and to take steps to bring it about.

THINKING AHEAD

This means having goals. This means having aware goals, clear-cut goals, spelled-out and specified goals for every area of our influence and interest, and for every epoch of the future.

It is best that these goals be flexible, subject to change by intelligent decision but persisted in against all fears and discouragements. It is best that they not be obsessive or compulsive but act instead like magnets or compasses, helping to coordinate and organize our thinking and action.

HAPPINESS

Happiness has been well-defined as "overcoming of obstacles on the way to a *goal of one's own choosing*." The rewards of having such goals are likely to be immediate. Such rewards need not be postponed until the attainment of the goals.

For rational functioning one needs goals in each of several concentric areas. One needs goals for oneself. One needs goals for one's family, for one's groups, for the community in which one lives. One needs goals for humankind as a whole, for our entire species. One needs goals for the entire world of living things. Finally, one needs goals for the universe.

LOOK WIDE

For reasons that can be traced historically, there is great pressure in our current culture to put the emphasis on selfishness, to constrict our interest and concern to spheres close to ourselves. "Look after yourself, don't mind the other fellow." We are told, "It's dog eat dog and devil take the hindmost." The present general culture encourages one to be preoccupied with one's own survival or at most the survival of one's family. This flows out of the historical fragmentation of society. It has its roots in feudalism, in slavery, in the desperate conditions of unplanned living.

Such short-sightedness doesn't work, of course. When through painful emotion one accepts limitations on one's interest in the survival of others, then one is in trouble. When one buys the notion, "I've got to look after my family, and the government knows what it is doing in Vietnam," then very quickly one is likely to find members of one's family drafted to die in a Vietnam war which sufficient interest and initiative on our part would have prevented.

Less common but still familiar are "save the world" recordings that produce obsessive activity on behalf of humankind to the neglect of oneself and one's family. Such recordings make one ineffective on all levels. Those who neglect self and family are not effective in their exhortations to their fellow humans for support on the larger causes. The individual who is a poor parent to his or her family weakens the effectiveness of his or her appeal on behalf of an endangered species or for rescuing of the atmosphere from pollution.

One needs goals on all levels at once. It is true that we are not able to do much about the Andromeda Galaxy right now, but it is also true that we will do better toward our immediate goals if we are aware that the Andromeda Galaxy is there, if we have an enlightened, rational attitude toward it and toward the rest of the universe.

HARD TIMES, HARD THINKING

In times of social crisis and collapse, such as the present, it is important for the welfare of the individual, family, and group that the great social situation be taken into account. One's individual survival requires that one throw one's weight on behalf of the emerging, healthy forces of society and against the familiar and imposing but destructive and dead forces of a collapsing society.

One needs to have clear goals in all spheres at once, then allocate one's resources sensibly to work toward each of the goals in a balanced, rational way.

LOOK FAR

As with space, so with time. We need goals for the immediate future, of course. We also need goals for each period of the future. We need to have clear-cut plans that we wish to accomplish today, tomorrow, this week, this month, this year, this decade, throughout the whole of our influence and functioning. (I refrain from saying during one's lifetime since it seems healthier not to regard death as inevitable.)

FAR AND NEAR AT ONCE

One can have the loftiest, long-range goals; but unless one has immediate goals, the long-range ones are likely to remain daydreams while the precious minutes of present time tick by unused. Lao Tze said that a journey of a thousand miles must begin with a single step. Having set a lofty, long-range goal, one needs to calculate back from that goal to the steps it will take to accomplish it, including what needs to be done this very day.

Similarly, to set immediate goals only without long-range ones is to misuse one's human capacity to really think and master the environment. Lack of long-range goals is quite likely to frustrate the achieving of even the immediate ones.

In counseling clients I notice over and over again that if one sets up an immediate goal of, for example, overcoming shyness by greeting and having a social chat with a person of the opposite sex, s/he will work on this goal only and will discharge much fear and embarrassment but will be a very long time in actually taking the step. If, however, in addition to setting the immediate goal of the social conversation, s/he also sets a long-range goal of having and raising a fine family, then this long-range goal places greater urgency on the shorter-range goal of a loving, dating relationship with a member of the opposite sex. If attention is directed to the long-range goal of raising a fine family, then the step of meeting and greeting a series of potential spouses tends to be taken quickly in spite of the embarrassment, with no diminution of discharge but much more activity toward the effective living of one's life.

One needs a well-rounded set of goals, complete in the immediate future and in the longest range of time. One requires goals for one's own individual needs and for every layer of one's groups and associations out to the farthest reaches of the universe. These goals belong in writing on the wall, written on the shaving mirror in soap, pledged publicly to one's counseling group, written in the charts of one's community class manual, publicly admitted to.

MECHANICAL ASSISTANCE

One needs aids in remembering what goals one is working towards and what steps need to be taken. A goal chart such as you will find on the following page will be helpful.

The struggle will be to keep these goals in awareness *against the forgetting effect of the patterns*. The only defense that a pattern

MY GOALS

	NEXT WEEK	NEXT MONTH	IN A YEAR	FOR 5 YEARS	FOR 20 YEARS	FOR ALWAYS
FOR ME						
FOR MY FAMILY						
FOR MY ALLIES						
FOR HUMAN-KIND						
FOR ALL LIV-ING THINGS						
FOR THE UNIVERSE						

has to prevent itself from being discharged and overcome, once it is accurately spotted and a direction taken against it, is its ability to make you forget the direction. To write directions down, to create charts, to set up devices for reminding oneself of them continually is essential to win through to full humanness.

FOR EXAMPLE

My goals for today, for example, are to finish the rough draft of this pamphlet and to have it typed, to complete the roster and arrangements for the weekend workshop which I intend to lead this week, to take my laundry to the cleaners, to call five good friends and co-workers on the telephone about important matters, to give a session to a co-worker who has been out of town, to visit with and be encouraging to my youngest son, and to stay informed about the world. My goals for this week are to conclude a successful workshop on the weekend, to help get a counseling module in workable condition so that people can use it, to confer with attorneys about setting up a foundation, to work on getting the family yard and garden ready for spring, to have dinner with my oldest son, to chair a productive staff meeting, and to discharge for (hopefully) about four hours.

My goals for this month are to get the remodeling of a building well on the way, to conduct an open question meeting in San Francisco and a week's workshop in Santa Barbara, to get at least one, hopefully two, pamphlets besides this one to the printer, to have a tooth filled, to keep my weight down, and to have a good conference with my cardiologist, as well as to spend an evening on the phone with my daughter and my second son.

My goals for the year are to move into and work effectively in a new building, to set up a dozen new Area Reference structures in new parts of the world, to become closer and in better communication with all of my family, to train fifty new teachers of Re-evaluation Counseling, and to emerge from an ancient feeling of not being liked to the point that I not only know logically that I am liked but feel liked all of the time.

My longest-range goals include the ending of the phenomenon of distress patterns among human beings. They include the turning of the earth into a lovely garden with the surface of the earth as a province of all living things in which we are careful guests, where our dwellings and transportation are underground, where the clean waters, lakes and streams are again full of healthy fish, where whales proliferate once more upon the oceans, and where clear blue skies and quiet, restful atmospheres make the earth a lovely place for the five or ten billion warm, loving people who inhabit it in zestful cooperation. I have a goal of all members of my family becoming dependably happy, zestful, and rational at all times and for all members of the Co-Counseling Community moving in the same direction and in the process including all the residents of the earth.

YOU
These are my goals. What are yours?

Unlittered woods, an unpolluted stream,
A fresh-swept hearth, one's body showered clean,
Soil tilled with care, tools in their proper place
Tell the real nature of our human race.
Dirt, smog, pollution, every form of mess,
These speak the presence of acquired distress.

THE USES OF BEAUTY AND ORDER[13]

As the successes of Re-evaluation Counseling have revealed more and more of the fundamental nature of human beings, it has also become increasingly clear that a human being's basic role is the loving mastery of the environment. Theories which picture the human being as at bay before a hostile universe actually reflect the past fears of isolated groups of human beings in danger from weather, disease or other hostile forces. Theories which propose the human role to be one of "adjustment" to the environment reflect undeveloped technologies of the past and usually conceal some rationalized appeal to oppressed people to accept social oppression.

Our past attitudes and actions toward the environment have been distorted and warped by the load of distress recordings that have burdened human beings ever since they became human. Yet even so, the human power to dominate the environment has shown itself clearly. Occasionally this power has manifested itself in positive activities (the clearing of stream channels, the terracing of mountain slopes) but more commonly this great capacity has evidenced itself in destruction (the extinction of large mammals, from the wooly mammoth to the blue whale, the creations of deserts such as the Sahara, and the pollution of soil, air and water as in the modern USA.).

There seem to be no limits to our mastery of the environment, but this mastery should not be expressed in exploitation or degradation. These are caused by the effects of distress patterns.

---

[13] First published in 1972 as a pamphlet.

BASIC NATURES REVEALED

For many years now we have had the opportunity to observe in detail the shifts in attitude and orientation made by human beings who have engaged in Re-evaluation Counseling. Such counseling consists of the systematic removal of the distress patterns which have occluded and distorted the intelligence of all human beings until now. Experience over many years has made abundantly clear that an unenforced, undistressed, knowledgeable human being's attitude and role toward the environment would be loving mastery.

MANY REASONS

There are many reasons for thoughtful care of our environment. We are absolutely dependent on our planet for habitation, support and nurture. We are able to exist only because there are continents, oceans, and atmosphere. Our lives depend on the thin film of life that covers the surface of our world.

The effects of past careless use and current mismanagement of the splendid resources of the earth are confronting us in our poisoned air, polluted water, and exhausted resources. Our actual survival necessitates clear thinking on the part of all human beings about these matters.

AWARENESS IS GROWING

At the present time we are witnessing and participating in a growing awareness that the care and tending of our lovely "spaceship garden" must become an ever-present concern in everything we do, as individuals and as a society.

The environmental crisis is forcing us to recognize our own role as the masters of the universe. Painful emotional experiences in the human past have perpetuated themselves as distress recordings that tell us we are helpless victims before a hostile environment. These myths are currently being dissipated by the reality of the overwhelming control and domination of the entire globe by our species.

A few years from now we will undoubtedly see detailed recycling of every resource of the earth which we touch. No air will be used without being returned to the atmosphere in good condition. Water taken from aquifer or stream will be returned pure. No bit of metal, wood, rock, or soil will be used without being restored to a healthy and useful condition after our use of it. The sewage and garbage of the future will be composted as fertilizer and humus.

Our responsibility for the whole of the universe is important but will be discussed in detail elsewhere.

THE IMMEDIATE ENVIRONMENTS

I address here the familiar area of housekeeping—the attention to our immediate daily environments reaching from our inner skins out for a few hundred feet. Because this close-at-hand area is where human distress patterns have "come home to roost," have "fouled our nests," we will not be able to come to grips well with the totality of our environment until we have achieved clear understanding of a program for and success in moving on the housekeeping area which lies close at hand.

The application of loving mastery to each person's *immediate* environment, to the details of everyday living, is important to one's own rate of progress toward being fully rational. It can be crucial toward making that time of progress rewarding in itself, not just a period of effort sustained by a hope of a rewarding future.

CULTURAL CONDITIONING INEFFECTIVE

Our culture has rigidly urged "good habits" of housekeeping upon us, but it has not offered us meaningful reasons or explanations of their importance. The results have been that, except for rare individuals who have intuitively reached an understanding of their role in this regard, most of the population function as compulsive messmakers, or compulsive cleaner-uppers with some individuals alternating between the two roles. Because we have not understood the reasons for it, the care of our immediate environment has come to be regarded as a chore, or as a duty at best, to be postponed or avoided if possible.

All of us have been urged to keep our skins clean, our hair trimmed and well arranged, our teeth brushed, our shoes polished, our clothes clean and pressed. We have been urged to wear attractive clothing, to keep the floor swept, the ring out of the bathtub, the dishes washed, the windows cleaned, the lawn trimmed, the sidewalk swept, and such other indications of a well-cared-for environment. We have not been helped to understand why these things matter.

We can take a fresh look at these reasons from the standpoint of Re-evaluation Counseling, that is, from our understanding of the difference between the creative intelligent behavior of the inherent human being and the rigid uncreative behavior of the distress patterns which afflict the human being (from distress experiences which have not been thoroughly discharged). It is then possible to look at our care of the environment with understanding and insight and to integrate our functioning in this regard with overall joyful and creative living.

RATIONAL REASONS FOR CARE

Why care for the beauty and order of our surroundings?

The cared-for environment is safer. (Spilled water or grease which is not wiped up can do real injury to a skidding human being.)

The cared-for environment is rewarding. Work, that essential function of the human being, is more productive and satisfying in a well-cared-for environment. (The work bench whose tools and materials are in order, clean, and sharp enables the serious worker or the hobbyist to accomplish far more in a given time.)

The cared-for environment is supportive. (Sewage and garbage, composted and returned to the land, provide rich sustenance for human beings and other living things. Unmanaged, they make our surroundings intolerable.)

The cared-for environment is aesthetically satisfying. This is important because of its broad, complex, and profound effects upon our individual and group ability to function. Let us examine this in more detail.

We are in continual interaction with the environment. Not only do we give signals out to it and continuously take action affecting it, but signals come back to us from it. The environment communicates to us through many channels. These signals say a great deal to us about *ourselves* even if we are usually unaware of the process.

The trim, clean, well-ordered, and well-tended environment tells us that we are functioning well. It tells us with a thousand signals that we are beneficent, intelligent, caring, effective and able persons. The immediate environment acts as if it were a mirror. If it reflects thoughtfulness, intelligence, skill, and achievement, then we are continually validated. We receive an accurate picture of our real human selves.

If the environment around us is disordered, dirty, and disorganized, unkempt, unrepaired, and ugly, then the messages from it tend to restimulate and confirm negative thoughts and feelings about ourselves which we have had recorded upon us by the invalidating experiences of our distressed past. If our socks and skin are unwashed, our hair uncombed, if the floor is unswept, if our "dishes are dirty and some in the bed," then it is very difficult for us to get a clear picture of our real nature. It will remain difficult until we have made the effort to clean up the environment and restore it to functioning order.

Personal neatness and clean clothes are signals to ourselves that *we* care about us, that we regard ourselves as deserving of appreciation and good treatment. Care about our food, not in pattern terms that we "deserve" one more sweet or overindulgence in rich foods, but in terms of the finest nourishment of just the right amount, is appreciation of the beautiful bodies through which our elegant minds operate. Exercise and rest too, so neglected in our United States culture, are part of care for ourselves.

CARE NOT CAMOUFLAGE

Such care is real self-appreciation. This is quite different from commercially restimulated urges to use cosmetics to paint screens over ourselves. We may intend to hide our patterned negative feelings about ourselves, but the result is that we hide what we really look like. We drench ourselves with perfumes in embarrassment and apology for our own naturally attractive human smell.

CARING WHEN DIFFICULT

Poverty is a powerful negative force towards disorder and discouragement. The destruction of life in modern ghettos and slums is in large part a function of littered streets, filthy hallways and disintegrating dwellings. If well-to-do but thoughtless people would criticize the slum-dwellers' failure to improve their environment, they need only live in such an environment for a few weeks to realize the terrible weight of hopelessness and discouragement that oppresses residents there. For the individual slum-dweller, however, poverty must not become an excuse to succumb to the pressures of discouragement and give up on improving the environment. There are many examples of cultures where neatness, cleanliness and fastidious care of the environment have been accomplished in spite of terrible poverty by agreement among the members of the population that these values must be maintained. The fight for beauty and order should be persisted with in even the most discouraging surroundings as a weapon for morale and for winning changes.

EFFECTIVE CHANNEL FOR STRUGGLE

Slum-dwellers cannot wait passively for a sense of fairness or human responsibility to appear in the halls of government and business and act to move them to decent housing or to renovate the slums around them. It is not the slum-dwellers' *fault* that they are in the slums but in the essential nature of human beings it is *their responsibility to do something* about change. Fierce struggle will undoubtedly be required in many channels, but one of the channels of such struggles is for the means for slum-dwellers themselves to clean up the slums. Direct participation by the slum-dweller in cleaning up conditions will not distract from essential political struggle on other issues but will act to rally and mobilize neighborhood forces. It will make it easier to win important allies from other sections of the population for the larger struggle.

THE WHOLE PICTURE

Tolerated messy surroundings not only deceive us about our own natures, they also communicate a false picture of reality as a whole. If we accept being surrounded by messes we are likely to begin taking the universe to be a mess. We are likely to begin to believe that reality is full of contradictions, ugliness, and hopelessness that are not really there at all.

It is not that nature untouched is beautiful while human effects are always ugly. This is not so. The essential beauty and order of the universe comes to us not only in the vast ocean or the untamed forest but it also appears in well-cultivated farm land, in beautiful architecture, or in a comfortable, well-planned kitchen.

The human-managed universe is harmonious when it is human *intelligence* that is doing the managing. Only that temporary kink in the fabric of the universe, which is the *distress pattern afflicting the human,* creates disharmonious function in the human being. Only this projects disharmony and ugliness on the human's surroundings.

MORE THAN NEATNESS

If the environment is merely neat, clean, well-scrubbed, and in order, it is not yet a sufficiently clear mirror of our own real natures. Our environment should remind us of our intelligence and our elegance.

The essence of humanness is *creativeness,* our ability to synthesize *new* responses. Our environments should always display, in clear view, evidence of human creativity in general and our own creativity in particular.

The leisured class of Golden Age Greece believed that every item of the human environment, every artifact of living, should be beautiful and unique. We see in modern Japan how elegance is sought in simple things, in the ways that rice is cooked, in the spray of flowers for the corner of the poorest room, in the plaited rice straw in which five eggs are tied together for the market.

CREATIVITY EVERYWHERE

The rich, creative complexities of music can be part of every human environment. Not only is elaborate hi-fi equipment (or a cheap radio) a powerful tool for keeping these rich signals of human ability before us. Our own whistling and singing are handy and effective weapons against the gloom and discouragement of a restimulative environment. "Whenever I feel afraid . . . I whistle a happy tune . . . . "

The walls of a dwelling welcome creative and artistic decoration, not only a routine paint job in attractive colors, but also a work of visual art by the inhabitant himself or herself to enjoy and be reassured by.

Many of us have had our skills in visual art so invalidated that we are afraid to even attempt to draw or paint a picture. This fear, of course, will yield to counseling. With discharge we can begin not only to realize but to act on the truth that every human being is gifted artistically, in the visual arts and in all others. In the meantime, it is perfectly possible to take a length of wire and bend it into an interesting shape, then mount this piece of wire sculpture in a prominent position. It's possible to take some torn pieces of tinted or colored paper and move them about on a sheet of cardboard until the arrangement pleases the arranger, glue them in place and, with such an "abstract collage" mounted on the wall, be continually reminded of one's own ability to create beauty.

A poem or verse which one has composed belongs in plain sight to be read and looked at. This will be another signal that one is a creative human being and in charge of the environment.

The decor of one's living space may well include one's direction against one's chronic pattern. Such direction will be stated in a positive fashion and should be up-to-date and current.

ALWAYS NEW AND FRESH

Variety and change are essential for human existence. So we will paint *new* pictures, we will write *new* poems, we will "get out of our ruts" to do *new*, interesting things. We will explore new ideas continually. We will think new thoughts as part of our resonance with the forever freshly unrolling beauty and order of the universe. One of the uses of that beauty and order and of our contribution to it will be for the enhancement and enrichment of our individual lives.

GROUP CARING

To care for our environment *individually* is a necessary but only a beginning step. When we care for our environment and express appreciation and enjoyment of it as a *group* activity, our mastery enters a new phase, and our enjoyment is multiplied.

A CARING SOCIETY

When housework and gardening become social activities; when the end of littering and pollution are triumphant campaigns in which the whole population participates; when the planning and construction of a park becomes a people's project; then we will be close to the functioning of the future. We will be approaching that style of life where each of us enriches and beautifies our surroundings in everything we do.

ANTI-REQUIEM
Why

IS DEATH NECESSARY?[14]

Today many people are using Re-evaluation Counseling to regain their original human outlook and abilities. In the process they discharge and become free from much fear, fear that has been attached to a great many objects or subjects. Fear of high places, fear of suffocating, fear of the dark, fear of the unknown, fear of crowds; all these fears are familiar to human beings in their usual distressed condition.

The person who persists with counseling over a long period of time, however, the person who joins with the growing group of those who are seeking to recover their human heritage as completely as possible, at some point faces and addresses his or her fear of death. It seems that every human child has at some time confronted the actuality and possibility of death. This leaves a quantity of fear on every individual.

Sometimes this fear is "buried" in the person's mind and is kept below awareness. Sometimes the person becomes obsessed with the thought of death. Such an obsessive fear may take the form of irrational preoccupation with avoiding dangers or it may become a danger-seeking type of pattern, the "death-wish" compulsion which has preoccupied many psychologists in the past.

---

[14] First published in 1965.

FREEING ONESELF OF FEAR

This fear can be discharged, and it often is to a large extent. It is of great advantage to the individual to do so. People who discharge their fear of death will reap many benefits just as from the discharge of any other painful emotion. They become more alert, more aware, more intelligent. They function better in present time.

There usually remains a residue of fear and distress. A client may say, "Well, I'm certainly not preoccupied with dying any more and I can see one has to put one's attention on present time, but if I think about it very much, it still upsets me. It doesn't make sense to me that people have to die." The wise counselor refrains from offering any platitudes or soothing viewpoints. The counselor who says, "Well, we all have to go," is of no assistance to the client at all, nor is it any better to remind her or him of the Great Hereafter, or the Pastures in the Sky, The Last Round-up or any other euphemisms for the projected notion of a life after death on some non-physical level. The words the client seems to need at this point to completely shake off the fear of death or of dying is the confident word from the counselor that she or he *doesn't* have to die, that death *isn't* inevitable.

CULTURAL RESIGNATION

Few counselors up to now have made this assertion with much confidence because the inevitability of at-least-physical death has been such a truism in our culture. "Only two things are sure, death and taxes." "We all have to go someday." The Rubiyat says, "And he who husbanded the golden grain, and he who flung it to the winds like rain, Alike to no such aureate earth are turned, As buried once men want dug up again." Some ultimate democracy is continually being ascribed (and not only by the poet) to the "inevitable" state of death.

DARE TO SPECULATE

Let us be very brave and actually dare to ask the question, "Is death so inevitable or necessary as we have assumed it is?" Many people will have intense feelings that this question should not be seriously discussed, but feelings are, after all, just feelings. Intense feelings can hardly justify avoidance of discussion or speculation. It may be true, as a student of mine once said, that a great deal of organized religion would lose its reason for being if we were ever to conclude that death is avoidable. Yet people who take their religion rationally are not likely to flee from discussing the question for that reason. If religion has a value, it must have a better value than being a comfort against inevitable disaster, there must be something more meaningful in it than a mystical reassurance against the fear of death. To speculate on the possibility that death is unnecessary is not really going to endanger anyone.

SURFACE APPEARANCES NEGATIVE

At first glance the evidence would seem to confirm the inevitability of death. All multicellular living creatures, both plants and animals, seem to have a built-in death mechanism that brings their individual existence to a close. A redwood tree lives a few thousand years, some insects live just a few days, but each living complex seems to come to an end. Most individual single-celled creatures die also.

Further, the very existence of life seems to be dependent upon the phenomenon of death. All creatures nurture themselves on the deaths of others, often simply by treating the others as prey, as food to be consumed. Even in the case of the green plants who make their own food and ultimately food for all the other creatures, the death of other plants and animals returns nutrient material to the soil or water which makes possible the plant's growth. We human beings exist on the top of a pyramid of life in which all forms below us consume those below them and in turn furnish food for the ones above them.

Actually, the evolutionary emergence of humankind was certainly dependent on a situation involving the death of living creatures. Only the death of the individual plus the continued existence of the individual's descendants has made evolution possible. Continual turnover of individuals is necessary for mutations to occur, for new forms of life to appear, for simple creatures to give rise to more complex creatures.

DEATH USEFUL ON PRE-RATIONAL LEVEL

In this sense one can say that death has been useful and necessary in the development of living creatures. Only this turnover has allowed life to develop into the complex forms with which we are familiar, with whom we are associated and from whom we are descended.

Individual living creatures other than human beings are unable to create new and better responses to new environmental situations within their individual lifetimes because each must operate on an inherited list of responses which it cannot improve in any creative sense but which can only be damaged or warped in some way. Given the mechanism of the death of the individual, however, and the proliferation of its descendants, then it is possible for improvements to occur in new generations. It becomes possible for life to evolve and assume the complex forms which it has reached.

RATIONALITY CHANGES THE PICTURE

Sometime in the past, rational behavior finally evolved. Members of our species have this ability (in far greater amounts than we have previously been able to use). We can come up with new responses to new situations without waiting for the slow mechanism of mutation and evolution to produce such new responses. Individual human beings are able in their lifetimes (in fact every instant of their lifetimes) to flexibly create a new, accurate response for each new situation which they face in their surroundings.

At this point, is death necessary? Does the death of the individual serve any useful purpose in the development of life's greater ability to take charge of and master the environment?

DEATH OF RATIONAL BEINGS USELESS

I think we will have to say no. As far as our observations have shown, individual humans are capable of coping with and mastering any situation which they are likely to confront as long as they are able to function in a human way on their own inherent rational nature.

Human individuals in favorable circumstances have shown evidence of this. The longer they live, the more they learn, as long as they are functioning well. The wiser they are, the more valuable they are, the better they can live.

What human beings are good at, at being human, at coping with the environment in a variety of masterful ways, seems to improve with experience and wisdom, with the acquisition of new knowledge and skills. Aging and death have interrupted this process for all human beings in the past but not to any useful purpose.

NEGATIVE RATIONALIZATIONS PERSIST

It will be argued that death is still necessary, that aging and death are still useful to humans as a race because "there comes a time when it is good to die," "it is good to grow old." It is certainly good to grow wise, good to acquire new experiences, but it is not good to age in the usual sense of having our bodies lose their effectiveness in functioning. Given the distresses of a bad old age, death is extolled as a merciful release, but this does not at all justify the combination of aging and death. If aging could be avoided, then death would lose its justification.

Again, it will be pointed out that we "lose our faculties" as we grow older, we become senile, we become too difficult, we're a burden on others. We will be told that there will be a time for us to "go home to our heavenly father" who (it is assumed) has either infinite patience with our senile behavior or has the mechanisms on hand to remove it and deal with it.

DISTRESSES CAN BE ELIMINATED

These injunctions are ridiculous in the light of what we have learned about Re-evaluation Counseling. The mental decrepitude, the increasing amount of irrational behavior which we associate with old age is simply the pile-up of distress patterns. We already know that this pile-up is completely unnecessary, that it can be reversed and can probably be avoided for the generations of the future. We can stay rational and not be the victims of this mechanism. We can avoid the distress recordings accumulating on us from our experiences of distress that we have not been allowed to discharge.

ARE WE STILL DEFEATED?

Suppose we are granted all this. Suppose it is agreed that, knowing what to do, we can free ourselves from distress and prevent distress experiences from accumulating on children. If it is granted that we would be better and better people if we could live forever then are we caught in a tragedy? With the possibility and the capacity for immortal life are we to be denied it because of the physical mechanism of aging and death which we apparently share with all other complex creatures?

PRESENT LIFE SPANS FORESHORTENED

Here we must speculate, but I think we can speculate with intelligence. My guess is that the mechanism of aging and death can be eliminated. We bear it around with us as a kind of inherited anachronism, inherited from pre-rational ancestors and ill fitting our own rational nature. Few if any human beings ever live to a natural old age. Even allowing the present biological mechanisms of aging and death it seems quite plain that most human beings die, not for "natural" reasons but because of the accumulation of distress patterns with the resulting physical deterioration. "Psychosomatic" ailments certainly comprise the vast majority of human illnesses, and these ailments, taking over the human, have a lot to do with aging and death as we presently endure them.

There are many indications that if counseling is applied thoroughly to remove and prevent the distress recordings from accumulating upon a person, that a "natural" old age would not begin for a human being until past 100 years. Perhaps a "natural" time of death would be in the 130s or 140s. We are not alone in speculating to this point; the increased life expectation which modern health measures have brought to the population is in evidence all around us.

ALL THE WAY

If we apply counseling fully and the aging and death mechanism persists, then will we simply age and die at a later date than we are presently used to? Must we still accept physical mortality? Can we have a prolonged but still only a limited life? Here, too, I think we can say, probably no. *We should be able to become physically immortal.*

KEY LIES IN ONE-CELLED EXISTENCE

The process of aging and death seems to be a built-in part of the pattern of development of individual complex creatures. It is infinitely varied from species to species, from kind to kind, even from individual to individual. Aging happens to the complex organism. It does not operate on individual cells nor on single-celled creatures.

Look at the fact of the existence of the cells of our bodies which are presently alive. Each is composed of living protoplasm, a very dynamic material. Each is the direct descendant of another cell which divided into two to produce the present living cell and another one. Each forbearer of the cells living at the present time had living forbearers, who, in effect, were the same cell. The two cells formed by the division of the single cell are actually the same protoplasm as the original. The descendant cell is essentially the same cell as the one which gave rise to it. In this sense, every cell in our bodies has been alive for well over a billion years. It has been continually alive since life first began on earth.

PROTOPLASM IMMORTAL

How can this be? In a sense all protoplasm has been alive, has been functioning as living material all through this period of life's existence, being divided into new cells in each generation of cells. *It must have been alive ever since life began or it could not be alive now.* If there had been any break in the continuity of that protoplasm's existence as living material it would not be here today.

So every living cell in our body has been continuously alive for a vast period of time, has lived throughout the existence of life on earth. This living material has not aged and died over a period of a billion years or so. Why must it inevitably age and die in a few more years? Is there some magic timetable that must operate to allow it to live over that period of time and then snuff out its existence on our death date?

THE CELL'S ENVIRONMENT

Of course not. What happens in the aging and death of individual complex creatures is simply that the internal conditions in which the cells of the complex creature live change so that instead of reproducing faster than they are worn out (which now happens in our youth and growth period), or at the same rate as they are worn out (which happens in our brief stable maturity), the cells do not reproduce and divide as fast as they are worn out, as fast as they are used up by the complex processes of the whole organism.

Aging seems to be primarily a process of running short of cells. The cells do not divide rapidly enough to produce new ones at a rate sufficient to keep vigor. The tissues run short of cells, they waste, they perform their functions poorly and at some point the complex interactions of the tissues break down and death occurs.

Why do the cells stop reproducing themselves at a rate sufficient for continued physical vigor of the individual? *Necessarily because something in the environment of the cells has changed.* Some environmental condition of the inside of the body of the human has altered to interfere with their capacity to reproduce at a rate to maintain vigor.

APPLY INTELLIGENCE TO THE PROBLEM

Altering of the environmental condition of the inside of the body is something we already know a great deal about. We correct all sorts of minor lacks or imbalances in the internal body environment. The person with diabetes takes insulin so that the tissues can function. The person with heart disease of a particular type takes another kind of medication that repairs the lack in the environment. Hormones and pacemakers, plastic valves and glucose are regularly inserted into human bodies. With the current advances in biochemistry and the present rate of progress in determining the structure, function, and interaction of the various materials which make up the human chemical system it should not be very long at all before information is available as to exactly what these changes and conditions in the internal environment of the body are that produce the aging process which culminates in death. Once it is determined the correction of it should swiftly fall within the capacity of human knowledge and ability.

CLUES EXIST

We already know of striking examples of recovery of youthful appearance. Certain rejuvenations are accomplished by tissue transplants or injections of certain hormones. Sometimes the appearance of rejuvenation is presented by the development of certain malignancies in glandular organs of the body. The malignancy, apparently as a side effect, produces certain chemical substances that interrupt the process of aging and give at least some of the effect of renewed youth and vigor.

It is not unreasonable to suppose that with the acquisition of more knowledge humans may have within their grasp the possibility of indefinite physical existence. The possibility probably exists of remaining a healthy vigorous mature person for an indefinite period of time, for preventing the aging process from occurring and, incidentally, for preventing death, which is at present the usual culmination.

RATIONAL EXISTENCE NOT FATIGUING

Will we then grow tired of living? Will we do foolish things to bring accidental death upon ourselves? Certainly we will not if the problem of human aberration is successfully grappled with and solved. It *is* enjoyable to be alive except where distress patterns obscure this zestful enjoyment of living.

When distress patterns are eliminated from humanity as a whole, when they are gotten rid of and are prevented from occurring in our children, then there is no evidence that we would find continued existence anything but an increasing pleasure. The ability to cope with the environment and to be aware of it and enjoy it seems only to increase with our experience and knowledge.

ROOM TO LIVE?

What about overcrowding? What about the population explosion? Will we be standing on each other's shoulders, alive but miserable through overcrowding? There is not any real indication of this. The careless increase in population that has occurred sometimes and is at present occurring in so many parts of the world seems to be no more than the momentum of the previous desperate struggle of the human race to produce enough descendants for the species to survive in the face of the threat of disease, disaster and the irrationalities of war.

Gains in public health and medical knowledge have removed much of the threat against which large families were a defense. We are seeing a surge past what seems to be a useful rate of population growth in many places only because tension and ignorance prevent people from quickly understanding that new conditions no longer require breeding at a high rate for the species to survive.

Yet even though all people everywhere are at present still distressed, already the beginning of rational restraint on population increase appears wherever there is any leisure and security. When we have security and are well-to-do, our birthrate drops. There apparently is nothing in the human make-up that forces us to reproduce faster than our good sense would tell us is correct. We just have to have the chance to use that good sense. We have to have enough security, enough information at our disposal, and we can be trusted to come to a wise decision on our rate of population growth.

SOCIAL PRESSURES FOR DEATH

What about the social idiocies of war and capital punishment as sources of death? Even in our present distressed conditions humans are reaching social judgments for their elimination. Certainly the rational humans of the future will not participate in such ghastly nonsense.

What then of the "sacred" notion that people must die "so that they can go to a blessed hereafter"? Well, the existence of a blessed hereafter has been seriously questioned for a long time by rational people. The notion of some kind of life after death on other than a physical plane seems to have arisen only through dreams of the dead interpreted as their "spirits" visiting the dreaming person. This and the notion's role as a comfort to people who fear a death they intuitively dislike and feel is wrong is quite sufficient to explain why the concept of a non-physical life-hereafter ever came into being.

RELIGION SERVED A PURPOSE?

I think perhaps there is another reason, too. Is it not likely (being as wise and brilliant as we are coming to realize people are) that in some intuitive way we have always known that death was a mistake, that our nature was actually such that death should not occur to us? Is it not possible that gods were invented by humans in an effort to project their own real nature outside of themselves and outside of the obscuring aberrations so that it could be kept in mind as a goal? "Be ye perfect even as your Father in heaven is perfect."

Is it not likely that the idea of immortality put forward on a spiritual plane and in a mystical sense has been a projection of the correct idea that we really should be immortal? Has the notion of immortality been embraced because, being rational, death no longer becomes us, serves no useful purpose? Has "immortality" in a religious sense been an intuitively-put-forward goal leading us to the point where our knowledge and control of the environment would enable us to actually put an end to physical death and bring physical immortality to the human race?

HOW LONG?

How long need it be before research puts this knowledge at our disposal? Will all of us presently alive die physically and only hope that our grandchildren will be the possessors of this immortality which we came too late to achieve? I think not. Actually the key question has been the realization of the artificial nature of human aberration, the unnecessary and acquired nature of human irrationality. Now that we have this out in the open the technical facilities of biological science are such that it is reasonable for those of us now alive to set as a goal the achievement of physical immortality for ourselves.

SOON

Certainly, I would guess that if resources, financial and otherwise, on a scale such as were poured into the Manhattan Project for the discovery and construction of atomic bombs, were to be turned to the question of human beings' permanent survival, we would not have many years to go before a major breakthrough would be made. Immortality could become the possession of us up-till-now "mortals."

What we have always wished were true is true.
The things we've always wished we could,
                    we'll do.
The Universe belongs to us. We've all the
                    time we need.
There's just confusion to dispel, some powers
                    to be freed,
Some pain and anguish to be felt as out of us
                    it passes,
Some knowledge to be widely spread through
                    our Co-Couns'ling classes.
To the ones who guide this process our
                    attention's here referred,
Re-evaluation Teachers, key spreaders of the
                    word.

THE TEACHER OF RE-EVALUATION COUNSELING[15]

A New Kind of Communicator

The profession of teaching Re-evaluation Counseling is growing rapidly in the United States. The number of Re-evaluation Counseling teachers is doubling every six months in the present period (1972).

At any particular time a good job is being done by all or nearly all of these teachers. The almost consistent success of very new teachers is amazing. Yet, to be more aware of the specific functions of the Re-evaluation Counseling teacher cannot but help the teacher to do a better job. All of us feel the need of improvement, of self-examination. Let us look then as best we can, from the present backlog of experience in teaching Re-evaluation Counseling, at the role of the teacher.

The teacher of Re-evaluation Counseling teaches mostly by example. Students learn to counsel by being counseled, by seeing others being counseled. So the teacher is necessarily a counselor in practice most of the time, demonstrating techniques, getting discharge started for Co-Counselors to continue with, eliciting discharge from the students in the class and between class sessions.

---

[15] Appeared in *A New Kind of Communicator*, 1973.

THEORY ARISES OUT OF EXPERIENCE

Counseling *theory* is the summary and distillation of *experience* with counseling. It is a composite and explanation of the common features of the counseling that has worked well. We stress at every turn that there is no rigidity to the *application* of theory, that the basic principles have to be applied flexibly and differently in every session.

There is a real need for offering theory, but when it is done well it is not preached or "told" to the students but rather demonstrated. The discussions of theory which are remembered well by students are the discussions which appear in answer to questions students ask and even more particularly in response to difficulties which the students have experienced and which they bring to the teacher for help with a solution. As the teacher demonstrates the solution, eliciting discharge where the Co-Counselors had difficulty in getting it, the opportunity arises to present the summary and explanation of other people's successful experiences which constitutes Re-evaluation Counseling theory.

MOST TEACHERS SUCCEED

All manner of people with all manner of distress pattern difficulties still impeding them, with greatly varying levels of experience and with greatly different personalities have become teachers of Re-evaluation Counseling. These varied people have taught Re-evaluation Counseling successfully and have communicated the theory and practice well enough that their students have Co-Counseled successfully and become skillful Co-Counselors. Many of these teachers began with very little experience or background, very little mastery of theory, and yet, slowly and sometimes with great difficulty, they succeeded in doing a good job. The success of their students and their students' students attests to this.

Why is this so? Is the answer that teaching Re-evaluation Counseling is easy? Can one be less than rigorous with a subject such as this?

CONFIRMING EXISTING HOPES

I think not. I think the principle reason for the success of our teachers until now has been that we are not teaching the students something brand new. We are communicating to them, we are reassuring them that the attitudes which they have always really held themselves and which they have persisted with in some hidden way underneath all the invalidation and counter-conditioning, are really true. We are saying to people that the ideas that they've always treasured deep within themselves that human beings are good, are smart, mean well to each other and should be able to solve their difficulties and get along are sound. We are affirming their hidden faith that there's an understandable reason why they haven't been able to do well before. We are saying that there's a practical solution to removing these reasons and allowing humans to regain their human abilities. What we're saying in effect to each person is that the deeply held concept of themselves as good, intelligent, desiring and able to relate to others is the actual case. We are saying what they have always felt, that discharge is natural and good and should be encouraged instead of suppressed.

These students are, in effect, not having to learn something new, but are being reassured that their deepest convictions about themselves and their fellows are the real state of affairs, rather than the conditioned, negative, discouraging, invalidating attitudes imposed on them by the culture.

CORRECTING MISTAKES IN THEORY

I have had a number of experiences of making a first visit to a Community of Co-Counselors who had been taught by *students of students* of mine, Co-Counselors with whom I had no previous contact. Sometimes it was quickly apparent that the theory of Re-evaluation Counseling had been distorted in certain ways by the teacher's own distress patterns and that ideas had been taught as if they were part of the theory of Re-evaluation Counseling which were actually foreign to it and contradictory to it. What is reassuring is that each time I have had an open-question session with these students who have been mistaught, they have tactfully raised a question about the mistaken portion of theory and have asked, "What about this — — — — that we've heard in class? Would you comment on this . . . . ? It seems to some of us that this doesn't fit very well with the rest of the theory." They have accurately spotted the contradiction and held reservations against the mistaken idea in a profoundly intelligent way. This is very reassuring. Not only do people have the ability to hear correct things when they are said in a correct manner, they also intuitively recognize and reject erroneous ideas as their Co-Counseling progresses.

All of us in Re-evaluation Counseling commit ourselves not only to communicate correct theory well but also to a continual intellectual struggle to develop the theory further and to guard it from the intrusion of foreign and contradictory ideas which come to us out of our own distresses and with the distresses of new recruits to our Re-evaluation Counseling Communities (as well as from other theories of human behavior which have embalmed errors from the same sources).

Why do we make this sustained effort? Why are we willing to take time to engage in intellectual polemics as well as Co-Counseling sessions to reach agreement on a consistent and correct policy and theory?

THEORY GUIDES NEW EXPERIENCES

We do this because our theory, the summary of our experience, is the cutting edge of our advancing influence in the affairs of human beings, is the weapon with which we beat back the forces of irrationality, oppression, and other expressions of distress patterns in the individual and society. The efficiency of our effort, the speed of our success, the elegance of our solutions, depend in great part on the correctness and precision of our ideas.

There is heavy pressure on us from individual distresses and from the culture to take what is in effect an "anarchist" position, to assume that good will is enough, that spontaneity is sufficient, that ideas and policies need not be rigorously formulated nor battled for. To the extent that this pressure is succumbed to, difficulties proliferate in individual Co-Counseling and in the Communities. Enormous effort, wasteful and avoidable, has to be committed to cleaning up the messes, straightening out the spreading confusion and restimulation that arise from it when with correct theory we could well have gone in a straightforward manner toward the goals we were after.

From another direction, mistaken concepts and errors of theory impinge upon us from the distress patterns and from the culture in the form of over-rigidity. These distortions try to present the theory as a series of pat answers, magic solutions to any situation, as a notion that we can come up with pre-conceived answers to categories of problems, that good counseling means copying exact techniques from skillful counselors and following these borrowed techniques slavishly.

This distorts reality to much ill effect also. It's a mistake on the other side, but it's still a mistake.

RIGOROUS BASIC THEORY, FLEXIBLY APPLIED

The basic concepts of counseling deserve clear formulation and agreement and need to be followed rigorously. Not only do our experiences all confirm the accuracy of these concepts but deductive logic, beginning with the original assumptions of Re-evaluation Counseling, confirms them also. These concepts need to be adhered to and used carefully, and any distortions of them resisted vigorously. Their application, however, must always be flexible. Techniques always need to be developed afresh each session for each client. Otherwise we have set up a well-intentioned, marvellously clear, but nevertheless *rigid* pattern of thought and have belied our own concepts. We need solid agreement on basic concepts and complete freedom and independence and flexibility in applying them. This is the combination that makes our theory come to life in the activities and gains of the humans who use it.

The teacher of Re-evaluation Counseling appears before her class as a model counselor. It is true she lectures sometimes. She explains and answers questions and presents theory; but by her actions, she shows over and over again *that* counseling works and *how* it works in particular cases.

TEACHER AND EXAMPLE, NOT PSEUDO-PARENT

Great pressure will arise on a successful teacher to become, in effect, a one-way counselor to all members of the class. She will properly play this role in the sense that the student often understands what counseling is about from being counseled, whether from a demonstration in class or a quick session on the phone or in person.

She must guard, however, that she does not accept this role fully and attempt to become a one-way counselor to a large number of people. This role is simply incorrect. It is too demanding on the teacher and it encourages students to assume a false position of feeling helpless and inept and invalidated and waiting on help from the teacher who can solve the difficulty. It does not get across the fact they can solve each other's difficulties.

PERFECTION NOT NECESSARY

The beginning Re-evaluation Counseling teacher often feels terrified at the challenge of trying to function as well as the experienced teacher from whom she learned counseling. Yet to be a good teacher it is not necessary to be so expert a counselor. It's not necessary that a teacher solve every single student's problem in class or even demonstrate how to get every single student to discharge. What she *does* do is demonstrate that discharge is *possible*, that a solution of and the freeing of a person from a particular distress pattern is *possible*. She does this by performing the act in demonstration counseling. This implies that it can be done for the others and that they can do it for each other.

It is correctly the students' responsibility to help each other to remove their patterns, not to stand in line to have their turn with the teacher removing theirs. If the teacher fails to do a successful demonstration or counsel a student in the class effectively, this does not lessen the teacher's effectiveness as a teacher if her role is correctly understood. She is not there as a paragon of skill. She is there as one of the troops who has had a little more experience to show that it is possible to make Co-Counseling work and to encourage and help the others to make Co-Counseling work between themselves.

On this basis the Co-Counselors become responsible and self-respecting from the beginning. It becomes their project to *learn how to* Co-Counsel, not to imitate the teacher.

GAUGE RESOURCES CORRECTLY

A teacher who is tempted to take too many students, or too many deeply distressed students, into her class needs to be aware of her own resources, to think carefully how many students she can be a model demonstrator for, and what depth and kinds of distresses they have that she can handle. If she takes on too big a class or takes on too distressed individuals or individuals with patterns which disrupt the class, she's not being a smart teacher. To have a large class that does not go well contributes far less to the growth of Re-evaluation Counseling than to have a small class that is sparklingly successful and the word of which makes other people eager to get into classes.

The classes that grow and furnish their own recruits for the next series are the classes where the teacher is able to play a good role and the people are carefully chosen so that they can learn to help each other quickly and enjoy the process of Co-Counseling. These students bring their friends into Co-Counseling.

The large (or small) class full of difficulties which are only partially solved will discourage its members. It also sets a poor example. New students that do come in will tend to be like the old ones, that is, full of deep problems. It will be taken for granted from the teacher's establishing such a class, that that's what the class is for, to bring people with deep distresses for the teacher to handle.

LASTING INFLUENCE

A teacher will keep on being an example to her beginning students all through their development in Re-evaluation Counseling whether they attend other teachers' classes later or not. Her influence and model will continue to be of great importance to the students that she first taught. Her correct choice of students and their early learning to care for each other, to use each other's resource for effective Co-Counseling, become of great importance. Otherwise she will be oppressed by the weight of the collective demands for one-way help which the increasing Community of her students will place upon her.

THE RELATION OF THE RE-EVALUATION COUNSELING TEACHER TO THE RE-EVALUATION COUNSELING COMMUNITY[16]

The Area Reference Person speaks for the Community of Re-evaluation Counselors. Any teacher of a Re-evaluation Counseling class is, however, also, in a more limited way, a spokesperson for both the theory and the Community of Co-Counselors. Most people will secure their first impression and first acquaintance with Re-evaluation Counseling from the teacher of their fundamentals class.

The teacher of a Re-evaluation Counseling class is in a position to be an unrestimulative collector of the necessary funds for outreach and growth of the Community. She is assigned this function by the Community. Class tuitions should be set so as to adequately compensate the teacher for what will be a difficult and arduous job in many cases. They should be adequate to

---

[16] First published in 1973 in *The Human Situation*.

allow that 25% of the gross tuition for each class goes immediately into an Area Outreach Fund and a portion of that into the Community Service Fund so that the work of the Community can be carried on. (Guideline H.2. 2010)

The Re-evaluation Counseling teacher is a principal distributor of literature, pamphlets, books, manuals, tapes, etc. for the students and participants in Co-Counseling.

New forms of classes will evolve. New populations will enter our Communities. We will need special classes for young people, interest groups, prisoners, ethnic groups, disabled people, etc. A great lore of how-to-teach will accumulate, and this will need to be shared by Re-evaluation Counseling teachers with each other through such media as *Present Time*, International teachers' workshops, and *The RC Teacher*.

A MODEL AND EXAMPLE

The progress of the Re-evaluation Counseling teacher's own counseling will be watched carefully by students and would-be-students. "What you do shouts so loudly to me that I can't hear what you say" might have been said about the relative importance of the teacher's own Co-Counseling and lifestyle as compared to her lectures.

In personal relationships, in financial matters, in community involvement the teacher will be looked to for an example, and the more rational her students become through their Co-Counseling, the more they will expect to learn from her in these ways.

THE ART OF BEING A CLIENT[17]

Most Re-evaluation Counseling literature is written for the Co-Counselor in his or her role as counselor, and properly so. All of us retain spontaneous motivations toward being clients, however much these motivations may seem obscured by inhibiting patterns. It is in becoming an effective counselor that we all need detailed guidance and encouragement in overcoming the conditioning against discharge and against assisting discharge which our culture has placed upon us.

Nevertheless, most of the rewards of Co-Counseling come to us as clients. Our success as clients, that is, in discharging and re-evaluating our own distresses, is the primary factor in the long-range success we have as counselors. Skill in functioning as a client is of great importance. The following guidelines, extracted from many experiences by many people in being clients, will be helpful.

First, take and keep responsibility for one's self as a client. It is marvelous to feel the responsibility of one's counselor standing by when one is in the throes of heavy discharge; but in between times it is best to remember to think about and plan for one's own progress as a client. One will have much better sessions if one comes to them with an idea in mind of what one wants to work on, and allows even the most skilled counselor to fill his or her proper role as helper rather than having to try to plan for the client.

---

[17] Appeared in *Present Time* No. 5, September 1971.

Second, one should *act like a client during sessions and only during sessions*. One will certainly have many informal, short or telephone sessions as well as one's formal ones, but one should try to be sure that the other person is ready and willing to be counselor before one "lets go" with one's distresses. To do otherwise is not only unfair to and an imposition on one's counselors, but it will not work really well for the client over the long haul.

Third, lovingly *care for and nurture one's counselors*. People who can counsel one well are treasures, to be treated with courtesy and consideration, to be appreciated openly and well, to be given one's best counseling back when the roles are reversed (and, if one is not yet able to counsel them equally well, to be tendered babysitting, lawn-mowing, floor-scrubbing, or other valuable considerations so that the relationship remains fair and mutually self-respecting).

Fourth, *one should act during and between sessions so that any observers will be drawn to the use of Re-evaluation Counseling* by the example of how responsibly one frees one's self from one's distresses, rather than repelled by the carelessness with which one exhibits and dramatizes one's material.

To inflict on other people in the environment examples of how loudly or daringly one can yell, scream, curse or repeat words forbidden in childhood is exhibitionism and the rehearsal of a distress pattern and *is not discharge nor responsible counseling.*

A client will sometimes need to yell or scream in order to get discharge started, but the yelling or screaming is not itself discharge, and can be done into a pillow or out of earshot of others when it is necessary.

Wrecking furniture or counseling rooms or other destructive violence is not discharge but is the unhelpful rehearsal of a pattern. Violent movement is necessary for some kinds of discharge, but this is easily achieved by jumping up and down violently on a firm floor, with no harm to anything nor upset to the neighbors.

Warmth and closeness grow naturally between Co-Counselors and between members of Co-Counseling groups or Co-Counseling Communities and is to be treasured and enjoyed, but this is a private matter. To embarrassedly or defensively engage in embraces in situations where such embraces will not be understood or to blindly try to impose such closeness on others, who, through no fault of theirs, do not or cannot understand, is again exhibitionism, not counseling.

All persons not yet in the Re-evaluation Counseling Community must be treated awarely and with respect, must be communicated with on the basis of *where they are, not* on the basis of how *we* feel, or where we wish they were.

A Co-Counselor once summed this up by saying, "We just mustn't wipe our stuff on other people or think that will help us get rid of it."

Co-Counselors must endeavor, like Caesar's wife, to be above reproach in their relations with all other people. And because we are Co-Counselors, always growing and gaining, this will turn out to be not so difficult as it might seem.

Alone and dull, if I but seek and find
Attentive eye and ear and open mind,
Confusion clarifies,
Awareness multiplies.
I give attention and am paid in kind.

MULTIPLIED AWARENESS[18]

(Using Re-evaluation Counseling in a Group)

Re-evaluation Counseling is the giving of attention and support and listening by one person to another, in order that the person receiving this attention, support and listening can discharge the emotional and physical tensions left by past distress experiences. It consists of two or more intelligences focussing on one person's distress.

Such discharge allows the person to re-evaluate the distress experiences (with sufficient discharge, they can become re-evaluated *completely*) and become rational and relaxed where she or he has been irrational and tense before. The discharge is outwardly characterized by tears, trembling, laughter, raging, talking and yawning.

In the most common mode of Re-evaluation Counseling this takes place between two people, one person being *the person paid attention to (the client)* and the other being *the person listening and paying attention (the counselor)*. In Co-Counseling the roles are exchanged in sessions. This works well and is economical in the use of only one counselor per client.

There are certain advantages, however, in having the one client have the attention of a group of listeners. It is important that only one of these play the role of active counselor (asking helpful questions, directing the progress of the session, offering

---

[18] First published in 1969; revised in 1991.

directions against the distress); but the group attention of the group as a whole enhances the discharge and re-evaluation of the client. Generally in such a group each person will have a turn at being the listened-to client, and it can often happen that all members of the group will discharge together with the designated client.

The presence of additional listeners multiplies the awareness available to the client and acts as a powerful contradiction to most distresses.

SUPPORT GROUPS

The most common form of such group counseling is the *support group*. Support groups began in RC but from there have spread widely through the general population in several countries.

The basic content of a support group is that each person has a roughly equal turn of being listened to *without interruption.* Various refinements and additional characteristics can be added to this, but if a small group of people will make and keep an agreement with each other that each is to have his or her share of the group time to be listened to while all the others pay attention to the person being listened to and will not interrupt, it will be a refreshing and satisfying experience for participants even if they had been given no previous exposure to theory and had no previous experience.

Experienced Re-evaluation Counselors will be generally eager to use their turn *for discharge* and will, but people who have been given no theory at all, to whom the value of discharge has not been communicated or emphasized, will almost always "invent" the use of discharge for themselves. Talking may be the only discharge for the first session or two, or talking mixed with laughter, but after not very many meetings someone will spontaneously shake or cry, and, if they are not interrupted, the occurrence seems to be intuitively understood by the others as expressing the possibility of the others also discharging such emotions overtly, so that laughing, crying, shaking and yawning, as well as talking, will come to dominate the turns in the group. Then theory can be offered by the RCer or the group leader in response to requests for explanations by an eager audience rather than by "teaching or preaching" before they have their own experiences of it.

A support group needs a leader. It needs a leader on the most basic level, to remind other group members, when they forget, not to interrupt the person whose turn it is. For most RC support groups the leader will be expected to also serve *as a counselor* during each person's turn: assisting the client to begin and persist in discharge, unless someone else has been designated to play that role.

The safer the person who is being given the others' attention feels in the group, the easier it will be for that person to "open up" by communicating and discharging. A strong factor in such a feeling of safety is feeling *understood* by the listeners. Apparently for this reason support groups whose members share some kind of a commonality of interest or experience tend to function better than those composed by random assembly. Support groups may be assembled simply on the basis of residence in a particular neighborhood, or because of ease of travel to the common meeting place, but it is common practice to have support groups assembled on the basis of a commonality. Examples are women's support groups, men's support groups, young people's support groups, young adult support groups, working-class support groups, middle-class support groups, pipefitters' support groups, African heritage support groups, Chinese heritage support groups, "mental health" system survivors' support groups, and so on.

At workshops, support groups serve as a small, basic "workshop" within the larger workshop and are often grouped around the commonality of a common interest in a particular topic. Usually during introductions at such a workshop, people propose a desired theme for a support group, and a series of quick, straw votes determine which themes will have at least three participants, and the support groups are set up on that basis. If more than about seven or eight people want the same theme, generally two or more groups on the same topic are set up. It is sometimes assumed that people will then work only on their distresses which relate to the theme of the group, but in practice each individual almost always works on what she or he decides to during her or his turn. The common theme frequently seems only to enhance the feeling of safety in the group because of this common understanding and interest.

Some support groups are organized primarily around discharge in a particular direction, such as the complete appreciation of oneself. Certain commitments which have become known as the Frontier Commitments are very effective when everyone in the group works on the same commitment.

GROWTH

A support group can be, and in many RC Communities is, a principal avenue for the entrance of new people into Re-evaluation Counseling. The benefits of participation are so immediate that people can begin to "feel at home" with the use of RC at once and learn the beginnings of the theory from practice rather than from "being told." The question, "Whom would you like to invite to attend the next meeting of the group?" can be asked at every meeting, and, if the person proposed is acceptable to the other members, an invitation is extended.

Since to have more people than eight in a support group session lasting a couple of hours tends to make the turns somewhat short, a group that has reached eight members should, for at least part of their meeting, divide into two groups, meeting perhaps in adjacent rooms with one of the more interested and capable members playing the role of leader or assistant leader with the second group. After this functioning has been tested, the group should probably divide and the two new groups continue to invite new people until they themselves divide. This can lead to a growing network of particular kinds of support groups, and the larger numbers can greatly enhance the stability and resources of the Co-Counseling Community. Thus, if such a network of men's support groups spreads across a city, there is a growing, rich variety of Co-Counselors becoming available for the men involved, and there is a basis for frequent and effective men's workshops. Improved men's policies in the wide world and in non-RC organizations can result almost effortlessly.

A support group can take on some of the aspects of a class in that the group leader can explain, emphasize and demonstrate the uses of self-appreciation, of holding a direction, of individual commitments, and other counseling tools.

TOPIC GROUPS

There is a certain kind of discussion group which has evolved within RC that is very effective and avoids most of the difficulties which beset group discussions in usual human affairs. We have called these "topic groups."

Typically, the topic of such a "topic group" is proposed by any person who is interested in having such a discussion. In a large conference or workshop it is proposed to meet at a time that does not conflict with other agenda points of the large meeting. The topic, time, and Convenor (the person proposing the discussion) are posted on the wall or notice board. The people who attend are simply the ones who are interested in such a discussion. There may be many proposed topics posted at the same time so there will be a variety of choices for people. No one is assigned to a particular topic. All who attend will be there of their own free will.

The general rule at Re-evaluation Counseling workshops and conferences is that at least two people must attend in order for the report from the topic group to claim the time of the large body. An exception to this occurs when the report is about some particular kind of oppression. In this case it often happens that to begin with, no one else will be interested in discussing this topic except the person who is a victim of that particular oppression. In that case, even though no one else joined in the discussion, the Convenor has the right to present a report on the oppression to the whole workshop or conference.

The Convenor of a topic group posts the notice, arranges for a place to meet and convenes the topic group. The Convenor first has the group choose a chairperson for the discussion, and a reporter who will prepare a short (usually four minutes long) report to the larger body, and, if possible, a second reporter who will submit a written report on the discussion to an RC journal or newsletter (if it is an RC workshop or conference) or to the local press as a "letter to the editor" or the pertinent journal that is relevant to the topic of the discussion. The Convenor may be chosen to be chairperson or either or both of the reporters, but need not be.

The chairperson's job in a topic group is to see that the discussion bears on the proposed topic and that issues are discussed rather than personalities, that personal antagonisms or criticisms of other members of the group are not rehearsed, that no person speaks twice before everyone has spoken once, and that no person speaks four times before every person has spoken twice. These simple rules increase the effectiveness of the group marvelously.

WYGELIAN LEADERS' GROUPS

Leaders' groups (Wygelian type) evolved in the Re-evaluation Counseling Communities and are now widely used in the

Communities and in the wide world. They eliminate many of the difficulties previously arising in the relationship of leaders to each other, permit the release of a great deal of individual initiative, and meet the essential needs of leaders in their relationships with each other. The membership of a leaders' group (Wygelian type) consists of everyone who is operating as a leader or willing to learn to do so in a particular constituency. Such a constituency may consist of the Co-Counselors in a particular Area, Region, or locality or of people who share a commonality of occupation, interests, concerns, or oppression. The only functionaries for a leaders' group (Wygelian type) are (1) a Convenor and (2) a Consultant. The Convenor is a member of the group who agrees to keep an up-to-date address and phone list of the members and notify them of a meeting when circumstances indicate a need for such a meeting. (The leaders' group [Wygelian type] does not meet regularly but only "when there is something to meet about.")

A Consultant may be a member of the group but need not be. A Consultant is the most skillful and best informed Co-Counseling leader available to assist the group (within Re-evaluation Counseling it is often practicable to request the Regional Reference Person to be the Consultant or to have her or him choose someone to play the role). The Consultant serves as chairperson during the first three items of the regular four-point agenda and serves as counselor on the last item.

A typical leaders' group (Wygelian type) agenda will be as follows:

"News and goods" as people arrive.

(1) Report, without interaction or comment from the other members, by each member of the group on what each member has been doing as a leader of that constituency.

(2) An analysis by each person from that person's own viewpoint of the current situation facing the group's constituency, what is favorable in the situation, what is difficult in the situation, what opportunities are waiting to be seized, and what challenges need to be met.

(3) A report by each leader on what he or she proposes to do as a leader in the next period.

(4) A demonstration counseling session with each leader by the Consultant on "What's getting in the way of my leading well" with follow-up commitments to continue such counseling by other members of the group wherever possible.

A closing circle in which each member says what he or she valued most about the meeting.

Leaders' groups (Wygelian type) *do not* attempt to draw up over-all plans or check up on the performances of the members. They *do not* meet unless the members or the Consultant feel there is a need for a meeting. They *do* release individual initiative very effectively and they *do* provide for rapid training of new leadership.

Having more than eight or ten participants at a particular meeting can make the meeting unwieldy in terms of duration. It has worked best to divide the group in terms of the functions into two or more groups when this happens. (For example, a women leaders' group might split into one group for women leaders in RC and a second group of women leaders in wide world groups.)

FUTURE GROUPS

Other structures and procedures will evolve in the future. As they do, it will be important to remember that any directive counseling should come from one clearly designated individual while other members of the group only furnish aware attention. The use of group attention is a powerful and satisfying resource. The multiplied awareness of many intelligent listeners is a resource that will often overcome counseling difficulties that are otherwise recalcitrant.

THE ELEGANCE OF CORRECTNESS[19]

The point of being alive is to live, to live well, to live fully, to fulfill one's humanness during one's existence. This is placed before all of us by the nature of reality.

The principle obstacle to living fully for human beings is exactly the phenomenon of human irrationality. Previously, the nature of this obstacle was obscured by our lack of mastery of the environment. It was possible until recently, as long as our mastery of the environment was low, to think that difficulties in the environment (disease, weather, enemies and so on) were responsible for our lack of fulfillment. Now mastery has been achieved to the point where it's possible to see the phenomenon of irrationality clearly. Previously, we saw human irrationality only in its bizarre or extreme forms. Now it's possible to see it for the pervasive, universal, ubiquitous difficulty that it is, the only one that seriously interferes with our fulfillment of our potential as humans.

A sizeable portion of the population has mastered or benefited from others' mastery of the environment enough that grassroots developments everywhere seek to recognize human irrationality for what it is, to identify its sources, and to create a remedy for it.

---

[19] Appeared in *Present Time* No. 11, April 1973.

We in Re-evaluation Counseling, through accident and persistence, have discovered and organized a successful approach to solving the problem of irrationality. We have called this approach Re-evaluation Counseling. It began as an accidental experience, grew to a set of techniques, became a theory and practice of counseling, involved a substantial number of people, organized into Communities, took the form of a movement, and has now developed a theory of relationships, a philosophy, a world view, and a program for involving others and permeating the population with its theory and practice.

(There may theoretically exist other solutions, not based on discharge and subsequent re-evaluation, but we do not at this time know of any that work for any other reason. The approaches which rely on drugs and manipulation at best produce symptom suppression, and are actually damaging to the humanness of people. Humanist approaches which do achieve real gains for participants seem to depend on the accidental or incidental occurrence of discharge and re-evaluation whether it's noticed or not, whether it's given credit or not.)

Re-evaluation Counseling is by now a rich, complex, highly integrated system of thought. It is logically consistent within itself and with the world and universe around it.

The theory of Re-evaluation Counseling is still growing and developing, but not by taking into itself any attitudes or practices contradictory to those already part of its structure. There is often pressure to accept contradictory practices into the RC Community. People sincerely propose a mixture of other theories and practices with Re-evaluation Counseling. These proposals are well-meant. They come from people who have received some help from these other practices and may not realize the contradictions inherent in them.

We have every reason, however, to rigorously reject such proposals and practices and keep our Communities free from any such admixture, not only from a theoretical point of view, but also from a large number of experiences where attempts to hybridize Re-evaluation Counseling with attitudes contradictory to it have resulted in difficulties and setbacks, both for individuals and for our Communities.

Re-evaluation Counseling states its basic assumptions (The Postulates) accurately and clearly and proceeds to develop its theory from insights gained in practice but rigorously formulated to be consistent with these assumptions and with the other portions of knowledge which have grown in context with them. It is no part of Re-evaluation Counseling to take an eclectic or pragmatic approach, to gather bits and pieces of information together and put an overall description on them without checking to make sure that they fit with each other.

Sometimes Co-Counselors feel that Co-Counseling isn't working for them anymore. On examination, it has always been true that Co-Counseling hasn't been working because it has not been used, because it has not been understood or applied correctly. There is real point to our teachers getting the theory across, not only in its basics but in all its profundity and depth, its richness of help for even the most difficult situations.

Similarly our policies, followed accurately, lead to warm, cooperative, effective, loving Communities where the resources of Co-Counseling are more and more available in all their richness. Where policies are meddled with, we have difficulties in Community relationships and a great deal of time and wasted effort must be devoted to straightening them out.

The analogy I think of for following or not following cor-rect theory and policy is the one of taking a bottle of milk out of the refrigerator carefully to fill your glass, recapping it and returning it, thus furnishing a refreshing drink of milk and no difficulty. On the other hand, if one grasps the bottle carelessly and lets it slip so that the quart of milk splashes around the kitchen, the enormous labor involved in mopping it up and making sure that parts of it don't stay under the refrigerator to sour and spoil is comparable to the wasteful process of making and having to clear up difficulties caused by not adhering to correct policy or theory.

It is not that our theories or policies are cut and dried. There is a continual need for new theory being developed as we tackle new problems. There's a great deal to be worked out yet about counseling with children, for example, with minorities, with special groups of all kinds. The integration of women's liberation with Re-evaluation Counseling requires a great deal of thought. This holds true for other fields. This does not mean quarreling with or warping the basic assumptions and the basic theory of Re-evaluation Counseling, which have proven their soundness with many thousands of people over a long period of time.

It is true, of course, that people who cannot believe this may take their knowledge of Re-evaluation Counseling and mix it with other contradictory ideas as much as they please. They are certainly free to do this, but they have an obligation to the Communities and the people who *are* trying to make it work rigorously, not to do it inside the Re-evaluation Counseling Communities, not to do it with their Co-Counselors who expect correct theory and policy from them, and, above all, not to call it Re-evaluation Counseling. It's perfectly all right if they wish to make a hybrid of Re-evaluation Counseling and some other contradictory theory, and call it John Doeism, if the perpetrator's name is John Doe, but the name Re-evaluation Counseling is correctly reserved by the Community for activities consistent with the theory and policy that have been worked out through so many people's responsible and continuing efforts.

LEADERS AND LEADERSHIP[20]

Is leadership necessary in group activity of human beings? Do human beings need to have leaders as they act together, or are leaders a luxury that people could well do without?

ONE MISTAKEN VIEW

The traditional view in our society has been that leaders are extremely important, that leaders amount to everything. History until now is the history of the king, the noble, the prime minister, the general, the team captain, or the star, while the workers, peasants, privates, and the supporting players only serve as a backdrop. In the traditional authoritarian view, people have generally to be told, bullied, pushed and inspired by a leader in order for them to act effectively in groups.

THE MISTAKEN REACTION

In reaction to this there is today another common view as people try to find their way to a more human existence. This view is that leaders and leadership are in themselves evil, that they should be done away with, that humanness means having no leaders. This view holds that "everyone should do one's own thing on one's own," and that this would work out in the best of all possible ways. This view identifies any leader or leadership with the distressing experiences of the past when persons in authority used that position to exploit or assist in exploiting,

---

[20] First published in *The Human Situation.*

degrading or oppressing the persons under their influence. All of us have had experiences at least with authoritarian parents' patterns, and most of us have suffered under the economic domination of an employer or employer's agent, autocratic military command, or a dominating person who imposed his or her will on a group.

AN INTELLIGENT VIEWPOINT

What is an intelligent viewpoint? The reality of the situation seems to be that humans cannot engage in group activity successfully without leadership, that successful group action always requires leadership and leaders. Though such leaders or leadership may be implicit, covert, or very subtle, they are a necessary element in any concerted actions.

A NECESSARY FUNCTION

This is so because intelligent thinking, which is an essential ingredient of successful human activity, takes place only in an individual human mind. Collective judgments can be and are entered into, individual conclusions can be communicated to others and discussed and checked (a very salutary process), yet thinking itself must take place on an individual basis. If people are going to act as a group or as a community, at least one person has to think about the group or community as a whole rather than think of the activity only from the standpoint of a participant. The more people there are who think of the group activity as a whole, the more people there are who assume the responsibility of thinking in a leaderlike fashion, the better the results; but *at least one* person has to play this role.

To decry or deny this role of leadership is to let it go by default and insure difficulty, and, if uncorrected, defeat. No leaders means no leadership, no leadership means no policies, no policies means confusion and defeat of the group effort.

LEADERSHIP FUNCTIONS

What are the responsibilities, roles and jobs of a leader? First, to think about the whole group's goals, to be farsighted about the group, to clarify and communicate the functioning of the group endeavor. Second, a leader needs to play a responsible role (not a monopolistic role but a responsible role), in proposing theory and policy and in evoking the thinking and discussion and communication that are necessary to set and clarify such theory and policy. Third, it is a leader's job to insure that such theory and policy are carried out. He or she must fight for the correct policies and theories, must uphold the correct ones against the reactive pressures which will appear from individuals' patterns within the group, from without the group, or from the patterned culture as a whole, pressures whose effect is to dilute and degrade and render such a correct policy inoperative. Fourth, it is the job of a leader to encourage and promote new leaders, to continually assist other people to move into positions of responsibility, to keep all participants in the group activity moving toward awareness and responsibility. Fifth, if the group is to grow and include new people, a leader has the responsibility to guide such growth, to implement correct policy and actions with regard to growth. Finally, a leader must insist on realism and responsibility about resources and the use of resources, financial and otherwise.

LEADERS' ATTITUDES

What is a leader's attitude toward the *members* of the group or community? History offers many examples of leaders who despised the members of their groups, who arrogantly knew best about everything and enforced their attitudes on all the activity of the group.

There are also many examples of poor leaders who, confronted with pressures for wrong policies or theories, surrendered to them, allowed the irrationality (which they were chosen to guard against) to take over in the group activities and, in effect, provided misleadership.

The correct attitude of a leader toward a group, it seems to me, is to realize one's special role in relation to the group, and try to fulfill this role separately from the other roles which one will have with the group—roles as a member, as a participant, sometimes doing several different jobs. One needs to keep one's leadership role separate from the other roles one may play to see that each of one's relationships to the group stands by itself, not ever intruding one relationship into another.

PATTERNED ATTITUDES TOWARD LEADERSHIP

What about the group's attitudes toward its leaders and leadership? Parallel to the authoritarian type of leadership is the familiar attitude of letting the leader do *all* the thinking. "Nixon knows best what to do in Vietnam." Another familiar attitude of group members is, out of patterned resentment at all past oppressive leaders, treating a good leader as an enemy and insisting that because of his or her position, and in the name of democracy, he or she should not defend himself or herself against the attacks. To treat leaders as enemies is likely to make their leadership impossible, ruin them as leaders, or actually convert them into enemies. A guide to a rational attitude toward leaders might be that criticism should always be offered of policies, not of a person, and that when criticism is offered, a better alternative policy should be proposed, not just a negative judgment on the one that the leader is offering.

Group members' patterns may ignore, oppose, compete with, or attempt to supplant a leader.

It seems to me that a correct attitude for group members toward a leader or toward leadership is to cherish the leader's correct role, to support him or her, and to offer overt appreciation (especially necessary in view of the extra effort which the leader is expected to make).

At the same time group members need to be aware of any of the leader's blind spots or patterns or mistakes and act in these areas as a counselor toward the leader, helping him or her to take a look at his or her distresses and to discharge on and re-evaluate them.

CHOOSING LEADERS

How is leadership chosen? Even in the most structured social organizations competent or at least aggressive people tend to be intuitively or blindly pushed toward leadership. It's true that a very competent poor boy is not likely to get sent to officer's school, but he is quite likely to emerge as a top sergeant just from the very interaction of the soldiers in the company.

Aware criteria of leadership should improve the process for us. A willingness to be a leader needs to be joined with the ability to be responsible and the possession of wide knowledge and competence. A candidate also needs to be free enough of other responsibilities and tasks that he or she is able to carry out the effort involved in the leading role.

To be an effective leader requires competence, knowledge, good judgment, willingness to be responsible, freedom to function.

PATTERNED MOTIVATIONS

Since leadership has in the past tended to carry with it money and power and, even in the most democratic group, carries with it a kind of prestige that is greatly desired by many people, unprepared individuals sometimes nominate themselves as leaders or have others do it for them in the guise of democracy, of rotating leadership, of letting everyone have a turn. This sounds fine, and provisions for allowing new individuals to learn to lead and be responsible (assistant teachers, Alternate Reference Persons, etc.) are necessary, but to accept someone as leader unless competence is present as well as the desire to lead, is simply playing games with a pattern. To replace competent leadership in the name of democracy or rotation with someone who is not yet competent is to risk deterioration of the group program and activity. To find areas for people to learn to play leading roles and to lead is healthy and necessary, but to mistake pretense for competence in choice of leadership is a disservice to the group and its goals.

POINTING ATTENTION AWAY FROM AND AGAINST A PATTERN[21]

Effective discharge of our old distresses requires, under all conditions, that a large amount of our attention be outside the distress recording, while only part of our attention is in contact with the distress, aware of it, feeling it. This condition always tends to produce discharge.

If we do not have a major share of our attention away from the distress, we become "numb" with distress, appear "calm," and fail to discharge.

This means that under almost all conditions of Co-Counseling, our major effort must be to keep our attention from being swallowed up by the distress. It usually takes effort during sustained discharge to maintain enough attention away from the distress, or contradicting the distress, to let the discharge continue.

This is the role of the positive direction, the anti-pattern direction. Our distress material acts as a sponge or a magnet tending to soak up and engulf our attention in all kinds of confusing ways. Frequently our trapped minds will rationalize that the direction into the pattern or with the pattern is the correct thing to do, and we will spend time being confused and ineffective in our counseling.

At many workshops inexperienced people are discharging very well the first day or so. Then after two or three days many

---

[21] Appeared in *Present Time* No. 8, July 1972.

will approach the leader of the workshop with a common complaint: "I haven't been able to discharge. I'm still talking about the same material with no discharge. Have I cleaned it up? It doesn't feel good yet."

In these cases the person has become preoccupied with the distress material. Urging them to take a contradictory direction often meets strong resistance. They will insist, "But it *is* my distress about my father that has spoiled my life. I *need* to talk about him"; or perhaps they will say "I want to get to the bottom of this material"; or "I've got to get this stuff out."

These rationalizations on behalf of the reactive pull of the material sound very reasonable. They have one quality in common, however: they don't work. More accurately, the counseling doesn't work when these directions are taken. When such a person can be convinced to try a direction such as "Daddy was always a joy" uttered in a bright tone of voice, discharge begins immediately.

The fear that if we don't keep our head immersed in the distress material we won't succeed in discharging is just a fear. If we take a direction against the distress material, such as "All is well" or "That happened long ago," we need not worry that we are abandoning serious discharge. The distress material will follow us out into the positive sunlight and will melt (discharge) under the proper conditions.

Finding, following and holding a positive direction in words, tone of voice, facial expression, and posture is a dependable, and the *only* dependable, mode for ensuring that our discharge continues and we stay in good contact with the real world in between our sessions.

Each to the marriage brings one's hope of love.
Each hopes for warm awareness that will heal
One's childhood wounds upon a tear-soaked pillow,
Embraced in understanding arms. Each seeks
And yet by now is unaware of seeking.

Each yearns, and yet compulsively refuses
What one's beloved yearns for, cruel denial,
Recording of the times one was refused
When help was sought from others long ago.

So up the middle of love's blissful garden
A thorn hedge grows. Old patterns strike and
    tangle
And those who loved and reached are walled apart.
In every home, to some degree, a wall.

We've learned to let distresses peel away
And free ourselves, regain our humanness,
Resist conditioning and re-emerge.
We counsel well with new friends. Those we love
We find more difficult, their hurts confuse us.

With spouse there's greatest chance of most
    confusion.
Yet chance of greatest gain and most reward.
The thorn hedge can go down, the warmth come
    through.
Each can fulfill the other's hopes completely.
Respect and love each give and take, unwalled.

CO-COUNSELING FOR MARRIED COUPLES[22]

Re-evaluation Counseling is the regular, responsible exchange of Re-evaluation Counseling between two or more people.

Re-evaluation Counseling involves a basic relationship between humans, the use of which is necessary for optimum functioning of any human being, but the practice of which is greatly inhibited in modern society. This inhibiting is the result of a conditioning which is imposed upon all of us when we are young children. We are conditioned particularly to repress the discharge processes indicated by crying, trembling, laughing, expressing anger and yawning.

One of the most valuable and exciting aspects of the rediscovery of these processes is that two people can systematically free themselves from their limitations through the deliberate application of the counseling relationship.[23] To do this involves distinct and separate roles for the two people involved. The first person, sometimes called the *client*, talks, remembers, discusses, discharges, re-evaluates. The second person, sometimes called the *counselor*, listens, pays attention, encourages, permits and assists discharge.

In the period of time or "session" that the two are applying the relationship, keeping these two roles distinct and persistence in fully operating within one role are important to the success of

---

[22] First published in 1965 as a pamphlet.
[23] See the *Fundamentals of Co-Counseling Manual*, Rational Island Publishers.

the process. However, the exchange or reversal of these roles by the two people concerned in a separate later session is perfectly workable and is the essence of Co-Counseling. This workability offers dramatic hope for the re-emergence of humankind to completely rational behavior.

NOT EASY FOR MARRIED COUPLES AT FIRST

Many years ago, in the first series of Co-Counseling classes, mutual restimulation often flared up between spouses in class. This "upsetness to each other" was so obvious and so troublesome that it became a careless truism in the classes to say that "married couples can't counsel each other." This became accepted as an unchallenged principle and was widely quoted. New students in Co-Counseling class were told by more experienced students or by instructor that Co-Counseling with one's spouse was simply impossible.

Though there seemed reason for this attitude, in actual practice the married couples involved in Co-Counseling classes never did quit trying to counsel with each other. The need and the opportunity were both present almost every day of their lives together, and the attempt to use counseling was made intuitively and informally over and over again.

We know now that a lot of successes were achieved by husbands and wives Co-Counseling even in those days, but the successes were seldom reported and the explosive, upsetting failures always were thoroughly reported so the notion that "husbands and wives can't Co-Counsel" was not challenged theoretically for several years.

PRACTICE REVISED THEORY

The event that finally forced a second look at this negative stricture was that several married couples too remote from the Seattle classroom to find Co-Counselors easily, but knowledgeable on how to counsel well from individual sessions with staff counselors, simply, on their own, turned to each other and began to make Co-Counseling work. In some instances not only did they make it work but they made it work spectacularly well. Very important gains were made. Outstanding examples of successful Co-Counseling were set.

Actually, Co-Counseling will work between any two people. It is a basic human relationship that all of us are equipped to carry out well. The only factor especially inhibiting its use by married couples is exactly the mutual restimulation which inevitably arises when any two people live together and arises at a faster rate in as complicated and important a relationship as marriage.

SPECIAL ADVANTAGES, TOO

Along with the likelihood of heavy mutual restimulation, however, marriage presents several positive and important factors toward success in Co-Counseling. The opportunities for Co-Counseling between couples exist in much greater number than for people from separate households. Every opportunity for communication presents an opportunity for effective counseling. The deepest and most inhibited distresses are likely to be contradicted to the point of discharge by a warm embrace in bed with the long night ahead to talk and discharge in.

Motivation is a touchy factor in most Co-Counseling. If equal skills are not furnished and roughly equal benefits are not received, the usual Co-Counseling relationship tends to sag and be replaced. A spouse has many good and compelling reasons to wish his or her mate to discharge and re-evaluate, besides the hope of being counseled back. The family income, the happiness of the household, the treatment of the children, the success of the marriage can all be enhanced by one's doing a good job of counseling one's mate.

NOT DIFFERENT RULES—BUT GREAT CARE

Effective counseling between married couples does not require a whole new set of rules and techniques beyond those worked out for Co-Counselors in general.

What it does require is that these rules *must be followed with great care* because carelessness or sloppiness will produce deep difficulty much more rapidly between spouses than between Co-Counselors that have no other relationship.

Following a correct path in Co-Counseling and avoiding mutual restimulations is something like walking a very careful path through a bog: the person who knows the path and follows it accurately travels easily; but the careless traveler will be floundering in the mud unnecessarily.

Between two Co-Counselors who have no other relationship, the bog has fewer deep spots; one can often wander off the path and still accidentally be on safe ground. The Co-Counseling process will often work well even though the theory and techniques are applied somewhat carelessly.

Co-Counseling between two people who have other important relationships, and in particular between people married to each other, is like traveling over a very *deep, sticky* bog on a very *narrow* path. If the exact counseling rules and attitudes are followed precisely, the journey is highly profitable; but even small carelessnesses will bring intense difficulties immediately.

It is easy to see why married couples who attempted in the past to Co-Counsel even a little carelessly or who let their feelings distort theory in the slightest have concluded that Co-Counseling between spouses could not work.

RULES FOR THE COUNSELOR SPOUSE

The counselor of one's spouse must remain *counselor* all the way.

1. He or she listens, pays attention, permits and encourages and assists discharge.

2. He or she does not offer an opinion either during or after a session on what the client spouse expressed.

3. He or she, then and later, represses any impulse to explain or justify his or her own position on incidents discussed in the client's session that may have involved him or her.

4. He or she keeps a basic facial expression of interest and approval, watches that his or her tone of voice at all times is pleasant and uncritical.

5. He or she makes a special point to remember to tell the client spouse how well he or she did, to congratulate him/her on being a good client.

6. He or she writes a formal note to himself or herself to not bring up any upsets received in the client's session in his or her own session when the roles are reversed . . . (possibly three or four sessions later if judgment is used, but *not* in the *next* session).

7. Discussion and agreement on the broad, safe lines of counseling "against the pattern"[24] are important to reach before the sessions start and be refreshed from time to time. But if the client spouse "forgets" and lapses into negative complaining or invalidation of his or her spouse, the counselor spouse does not reproach, threaten or otherwise try to force the client spouse back on the positive track.

---

[24] See "The Complete Appreciation of Oneself."

The counselor spouse withholds any comment but in his or her own session sets such an example of being positive, holding to a direction and discharging successfully that the communication by example (not by reproach or lecture) takes care of the difficulty.

RULES FOR THE CLIENT SPOUSE

The client spouse, on his or her part, has much to contribute to the success of the relationship. There may be a reactive urge to dramatize at the counselor spouse, to complain, to air grievances, to "let him/her really know now that s/he's finally listening." This is *not* a good idea. The session may still work if the counselor spouse is being the perfect counselor, but it will not work nearly as well as when the client spouse, too, functions responsibly.

The client spouse should:

1. Remember to be positive.

2. If negative feelings are going to be described, reassure the counselor spouse before verbalizing them. Say, "Remember, these are just my feelings I'm trying to get rid of. Let me say them but don't take them seriously."

3. On heavy, chronic feelings, resort to contradicting them exactly. Say the exact opposite of the negative "thought" happily, out loud, several times. Hold this direction even during discharge.

4. Contradict all negative "thoughts" about the counselor spouse by saying the exact opposite in a happy tone. Refrain from sarcastic sounds as you say good things about him or about her.

5. Express warmth and appreciation for the session when it is over.

CORRECT ATTITUDES WON'T BE RESISTED

One's spouse will always welcome a counselor's attitude being taken toward him or toward her. This is what each member of a marriage has wished to have from his or her spouse as long as they have been married. Apparent objections will be echoes of past restimulations that will quickly die away *or* they will be warnings that *one's own attitude* is not yet that of a counselor.

The deliberate use of Co-Counseling can be integrated into daily life to a profound degree.

Homecomings need to be cleared for time for both spouses to take turns listening to the events of the day. A counseling student who had been away for several years returned for a visit. She spoke of her marriage and her spouse. She said, "When he comes home from work, he insists that I drop whatever I'm doing and sit down and then he tells me every single thing that goes on in his day, every person he talked to, what he said, what they said, every telephone conversation, every thought that crossed his mind and he doesn't want me to do anything else—get dinner, do housework, even answer phone calls until he gets done telling me every single thing that went on during the day." Later, she mused, "You know, I have the happiest marriage that anyone ever had."

Needless to say, this listening to the events of the day must take place *both* ways. The homemaker's day needs to be heard also. Flexibility governs in who listens first.

THE COMPLETE APPRECIATION TECHNIQUE

The technique of the complete appreciation of oneself has enhanced group counseling by removing the usual source of restimulation in group counseling situations; that is, the giving of directions by one member of the group to another. Now, in line with the complete appreciation of oneself, each person knows in advance how he or she intends to spend his or her turn in front of the group. He or she relies not at all on directives from the others, which while well-meant were often restimulative.

This is dependable and probably necessary in the formal Co-Counseling sessions of a married couple. Nowhere is the "helpful" directive more likely to be restimulative than between a pair of spouses. To hold to this commitment, to self-apprecia-tion by client spouse and no directions by counselor spouse, formally and carefully, will work as well and is probably even more necessary between husband and wife than in a Co-Coun-seling group.

It would be well for any couple who begins Co-Counseling to plan the first twenty or so sessions which they undertake to be based on warm, aware, approving listening on the part of the counselor spouse while the client spouse appreciates himself or herself without reservations, trying to keep posture, words, tone, facial expression in line with the appreciation.

AFFECTION AS A COUNSELING TOOL

We've known for some time that the expression of love is as dependable an avenue for contradicting chronic patterns as the appreciation of oneself. In many Co-Counseling or group ses-sions this seems difficult or "out of line," yet whenever a group has worked well enough and long enough together to be at ease with one another, the expression of affection has become an im-portant part of their group counseling technique. With married Co-Counselors, all formal difficulties disappear in this whole field because no one has a better reason or more opportunity or less embarrassment for expressing affection and love than a pair of spouses.

Every married person feels a lack of enough expression of love from his or her spouse. No one has really ever received all the affection one wants in a rational sense. With encouragement and purpose, the expression of love to one another becomes a safe, dependable approach for Co-Counseling as well as a great source of enrichment to all of the marriage relationship.

Love and affection need to be verbalized, but the tone of voice, expression of face and the general attitude need to be watched quite as much as the words. The person who, because of a pattern, says "I love you" in an embarrassed squawk is not likely to notice that he or she has not communicated love. The person hearing it, however, *always* knows the difference, *always* misses the undistorted love they wished to hear, *always* hears the embarrassed or frightened sounds which filtered it.

There is no limit to how long a time one can profitably devote to an aware and rational expression of love. This needs to be done verbally, but verbalizing is by no means sufficient. One's tone needs to be loving. One's look needs to be loving. One needs to touch and caress one's beloved.

For married couples, aware, loving participation in sex becomes a great gateway for emergence from chronic patterns of fear and embarrassment as well as an important enrichment of the sex relationship itself.

There is an old folk saying for married people which says "never sleep on a quarrel." A minimum activity for a married couple before sleep should be the exchange of affection, cuddling and entering into communication and the appreciation of themselves and each other. Where tension is present, a little time taken from trying to go to sleep to secure discharge will more than repay the effort with the restfulness of the sleep that follows.

FUTURE IMPROVEMENTS IN KNOWLEDGE

In the future as we become more and more skilled counselors I think that we can expect more and more Co-Counseling to be done between people who are married to each other. Difficulties exist but great opportunities and effectiveness and motivations exist also.

Certainly any person who intends to walk free from all of his or her patterns will not wish to leave a spouse still imprisoned within his or hers.

CHILDREN WILL PARTICIPATE

Children need, want and expect to be counseled by their parents. Once the parents have learned to Co-Counsel with each other the children become easy to deal with. Their patterns are not so heavy. It's easier for them to respond with love and warmth if the parent does the correct thing. The Co-Counseling parent will find himself or herself luckily besieged by children desiring an opportunity to discharge, to love, and to be close. When two parents have learned to conduct a small group session of appreciating each other and appreciating oneself, then the children are ready to be drawn in and group sessions will be better because they are there.

The explanation to the children needs to avoid big words. It's quite meaningful to say, "Let's just say nice things about ourselves, even if they don't feel true, even if they just sound funny, let's just see how nice we can talk about ourselves." The child, once started, will understand the theory with great rapidity and will tend to apply the good attitude and hold the good direction between sessions and in usual activities much more easily than the adult.

MORE ENJOYABLE MARRIAGE

Marriage has come to seem a difficult relationship to many people. The seeming enforcement inherent in the legal code of marriage, the restimulation of parents' patterns because of the similarity of the relationship, the strains of modern living, have all made marriage seem to be a sorry institution in a great many respects. Yet with the tools of Co-Counseling used systematically and deliberately within the relationship, marriage may yet come to be the state which religions and society have hopefully proclaimed it to be.

THEORY AND POLICY[25]

Newer members of our Community (and we are all quite new) sometimes are restive and impatient with insistence on the rigorous application of Re-evaluation Counseling theory in Co-Counseling. Others feel insistence on agreed-upon policy in Community affairs (the *Guidelines*) is too restrictive and interferes with the creativity and initiative which they hope to recover in their Co-Counseling.

Feelings, of course, are not a guide to action for intelligent humans. Our acts and proposals should flow out of logical thinking and should bear up under logical appraisal.

These Co-Counselors should be reassured, however, that there is ample opportunity for creative contributions to both theory and policy. Our theory is by no means cut-and-dried but is continually growing and developing. We are just beginning to learn how our Communities should function, and the *Guidelines* are explicitly subject to review and revision each year.

Novelty is not necessarily creativity, however. It is important that contradictory, unworkable practices and ideas not be introduced into either theory or policy by patterns or by undigested fragments of other disciplines. Honest mistakes are still mistakes. Well-intentioned errors still have poor results.

Re-evaluation Counseling theory is a rich, complex, integrated body of knowledge. It is a deductively logical structure (which few, if any, other social sciences have even attempted). Its

---

[25] Appeared in *Present Time* No. 9, October 1972.

assumptions are clearly stated and its theorems and conclusions are carefully and consistently derived from them, as well as being rigorously checked in practice by many Co-Counselors before they are included in the theory.

When new Co-Counselors, for example, want to mix Co-Counseling with some of the things they experienced in encounter groups previously, they may have the best of intentions and "good feelings" about their intentions. They probably were able to discharge to some extent in the encounter experiences and "know" it was helpful to them. What they may not be able to understand until they have more experience is that RC is designed to be helpful to *everyone*, not just a lucky few; that there is great good reason for RC to rigorously exclude the invalidation and dramatization that proliferate in encounter groups.

Similarly, some new Co-Counselors feel the "blue pages" policy (the rule that Co-Counselors not set up other social relationships with people they first meet in the RC Community) is an intolerable restriction on their "freedom." Yet one need only put oneself in the mental position of the spouse or parent of a new Co-Counselor to realize that this is a necessary guarantee and reassurance that the warm, open, loving relationship of Co-Counseling not be taken advantage of by someone else's distress pattern.

CREATIVITY[26]

It is the nature of human intelligence to be continually creative.

In the longer Re-evaluation Counseling workshops, individual workshop members astound each other by their ability to paint, compose, write, choreograph, sculpt, assemble and create in hundreds of ways. What people in Re-evaluation Counseling workshops present to each other on creativity show-and-tell night is truly a glimpse into the infinite ability and variety of the human mind.

Continual creativity is needed in our Re-evaluation Counseling Communities, especially where our theory and policy impinge on broader fields. We need to come up with thoughtful and workable answers and directions in the schools, in factories, in the scholastic disciplines, in work with children, prisons, armies and churches.

Creativity requires boldness. It requires bravery. Fears of anything new sit heavily on most of us. It is not surprising that, trying to be creative but in the grip of unsuspected chronic fears, we sometimes come up with distortions and uncreative notions in the name of creativity.

---

[26] Appeared in *Present Time* No.11, April 1973.

Re-evaluation Counseling has a rigorous, integrated theory which should guide all applications of counseling, but the applications themselves should be flexible and creative. The technique that is just right for the particular client or the particular session is the one that you *invent yourself* just that moment, not the one that you borrow from something you've read.

Novelty is not necessarily creativity. To introduce disorder and degradation into an ordered effort is to produce novelty but is not creative. To abandon responsibility, to portray deterioration and patterned behavior as basic reality, is not creativity. Creativity operates in an integrating, positive direction.

Understandably, people rebelling against existing negatives sometimes settle for other negatives, because under the conditions of our oppressive society, it often seems that to do something different must necessarily be better than going along with the status quo and the things that are obviously wrong (e.g., the "rebellious" decision to use marijuana instead of alcohol). The result is not creativity, however, except by sheer accident. To see who can make the most novel mess does not guarantee something creative emerging.

(It's always possible to take any disaster or any mess as a starting point, and from that proceed to achieve and integrate and grow, but that is a different process entirely.)

Variety is not necessarily creativity. Not all new combinations or variations are necessarily significant, and to be truly creative requires the creation of something significant. A mathematician, for example, given a set of axioms and definitions and undefined terms, can grind out an almost infinite number of theorems from them, but most of these will be meaningless and valueless. It takes intelligence (often operating intuitively) to conjecture which theorems are significant and to seek to prove these.

Not the making of messes, however new and strange; not the abandonment of responsibility simply because responsibility has become rigid in our society; not settling for mere novelty; none of these fulfill the requirements of creativity. Creativity involves something new and something significant, something positive, something in an integrated direction. At workshops we have a glimpse of how all of us can create well. With more understanding the day can come when every act at our hand will be a creative one in the finest sense, and men and women will rejoice in each other's accomplishments from minute to minute.

THE WAY WE DEVELOP[27]

All of us enter the Co-Counseling Community as clients. The progress of recovering our real nature and our occluded intelligence is a persisting and rewarding motivation for each of us in all our RC activities. None of us ever lose this need to be a successful client.

Each of us soon finds, however, that in order to receive as much good counseling as we desire it is necessary that we counsel others. Only this way is the total store of available counseling enough to go around. So we learn to be counselors.

Then we master the more difficult feat of *Co-Counseling*, of taking turns at being counselor and client with the same person. This difficult relationship is the hallmark of our Communities. We are communities of *Co-Counselors*.

Inevitably we find ourselves recruiting new individuals to Co-Counseling, motivated in part by our need for a greater variety of Co-Counselors and in part by the discomfort of maintaining relationships with families and friends unless they, too, gain in awareness.

Then we find it necessary to build *Communities* so that the relationships between ourselves and our Co-Counselors can operate in the most rewarding manner.

---

[27] Appeared in *Present Time* No. 9, October 1972.

Further, in the very nature of our progress we begin to permeate society and the organizations of society. By precept and by example we begin to change the relationships and behaviors of the individual humans in these social organizations in a rational direction. This kind of influence spreads far beyond the individuals directly involved in Co-Counseling. At some future time this will undoubtedly result in profound changes in the social organizations themselves.

ALLOW OURSELVES
TIME TO GROW[28]

Co-Counseling tends to be effective from the very beginning if people really make an effort to listen to each other well. For both client and counselor to pay attention to the client and to encourage discharge, allows the tremendous ability of the client's mind to throw off the distress and recover its vast potential to begin to operate.

There is a great deal more to learn that will help make these fundamental processes be more effective. This knowledge has continued to accumulate throughout the forty years since Re-evaluation Counseling began, but it is still in operation currently.

"Learning to Co-Counsel More Effectively" is an ongoing, permanent process and one that enhances our functioning and our enjoyment of living in ways that are very precious to all of us who have experienced them. The speed of re-emergence seems to be accelerating, but this will tend to be obscured from each person's awareness about himself or herself by the fact that our goals and ambitions tend to extend and become loftier even faster than our progress.

We need to be patient with ourselves about our progress—not resigned or discouraged—but patient. Re-emergence is a very complex process, and distresses that have been installed and restimulated for scores of years may take some time to fully eliminate.

---

[28] Appeared in *Present Time* No. 8, July 1972; revised 1991.

If every one of us had access to the very best counselors that we have developed, progress could indeed be dramatic. These very best counselors, however, have, universally and correctly, decided that they will spend much of their energy teaching other people to become teachers so the knowledge can spread. All humanity needs to be eventually involved in this. They also seek to exchange help with others on the same level as themselves as a step to preparing a large enough leadership body for the events ahead.

A large minority of chronic patterns are not sufficiently contradicted by permissive counseling. The directive counseling that these require involves finding, constructing and implementing "contradictions" to the contents of the chronic pattern. In the nature of the chronic pattern, the client will be pulled to identify with it and defend it. The development of enough confidence in the counseling process itself to risk accepting the counselor's guidance to this extent may take some time.

People who share a common oppression will tend to find some beginning safety in this commonality. Yet patterns of oppression can become internalized and accepted as reality. Or they can become rehearsed against others in a similar oppressed role. Thus a Co-Counselor outside that particular oppression will find it much easier to devise effective contradictions against such internalized patterns of oppression but may face a difficult task in winning the confidence of such a client enough for them to accept such help.

The whole concept of *contradiction* (we define "contradiction" in RC as anything that helps the victim of the pattern see the pattern as not present-time reality) has only partially been explored.

There are great areas of mistreatment in the current societies that are still largely unfaced. The physical mistreatment of children, both by parents and in the schools, was until recently "officially approved" by the society and its spokespersons.

The existence of a vast, seamy underground culture involving the sexual abuse of children is currently just emerging into the open. This is a phenomenon that it would be impossible to understand unless we had come to understand the mechanisms of the distress recordings and their perpetuations. The peculiar and distinctive sets of patterns installed upon the members of the different economic classes in our societies are still only beginning to be explored.

We have built what we call "Communities" to enable us to organize and keep in touch with the accumulating resources of Co-Counselors and knowledge. Membership in these Communities requires some commitment and dedication and agreement to try to eliminate the intrusion of patterns into our relationships with each other.

It takes time and experience to understand these things well and use them well. Sharing the precious insights that we have unearthed accurately and widely with others is a satisfying and rewarding activity, but is not always easily seen as such by beginning Co-Counselors. Assuming leadership is essential to one's full development and yet people in our societies have been subjected to enormous conditioning against doing so.

To summarize, Co-Counseling is an ongoing activity. It is not a substitute for living. It is not something to become obsessed with to the exclusion of other activities or enjoyments. Yet a certain amount of commitment, persistence, and patience are called for.

To attend a fundamentals class and have a few good sessions has seemed to some people to produce more changes in their lives than they have dared to hope for, but there is much more possible. I hope the reader participates fully in this promising future.

INVITING NEW FRIENDS TO CO-COUNSELING[29]

Wherever we live, we live surrounded by human beings, each one of whom is of great worth and enormous potential. All of these people will eventually be involved in what we call Co-Counseling or be influenced by it.

Among the whole group of the population are many very deeply distressed human beings. They are no less worthy, no less beautiful, no less essentially human simply because their hurts were piled deeper. It was in no sense their fault that they were battered even more than the rest of us.

Much more resource and effort is necessary, however, for them to win their way back to the point of becoming effective two-way Co-Counselors. We must have substantial surplus resources of time, attention, and counseling skill available before we can responsibly assume the job of involving them in our Communities.

This is not indifference or hard-heartedness. It is hard-headedness.

We will never lose sight of the fact that the majority of the world's beloved humans exist under burdens of deep distress from which they await a workable opportunity to win their release. The beginning plans for effective action towards this are already in the works.

---

[29] First published in 1972.

We would be foolish, however, to let patterns of sympathy, guilt or do-goodism blind us to the necessity at this stage of our development of recruiting to our Community people in the very best shape that we can find. We need to bring into our midst people who, given a moderate amount of initial assistance, become effective Co-Counselors without great delay and contribute their talents to our common store.

To bring deeply distressed individuals into our classes and Communities at the present time is to overburden our still scanty resources and from a long-range point of view delay rather than expedite the bringing of effective help to the deeply distressed.

If you have a friend, relative or acquaintance who is deeply distressed and you yourself want to take on the responsibility of being counselor to that person, more power to you; but you will need to face the size of the effort that you will have to expend and not try to load this effort onto the shoulders of others in the Community. It is no favor to the teacher of your Co-Counseling class to bring a deeply distressed acquaintance to the class because "he needs RC" nor is it really any favor to the individual himself or herself.

Whom should we invite into the Co-Counseling Communities and classes? The sharpest people we know. The ones we would be delighted to have as Co-Counselors. The ones that will help us accumulate the collective resources and the organized structures to eventually meet the needs of the deeply distressed.

Re-evaluation Counseling Publications

Books

The Human Side of Human Beings
An Unbounded Future
The Kind, Friendly Universe
A Better World
Start Over Every Morning
The Longer View
The Rest of Our Lives
The Reclaiming of Power
The Benign Reality
The Upward Trend
The Human Situation
"Quotes"
Harvey Jackins Memorial
The List
Fundamentals of Co-Counseling Manual
A New Kind of Communicator
Rough Notes from Calvinwood I
Rough Notes from Buck Creek I
Rough Notes from Liberation I & II
Counselor's and Client's Notebooks
Zest Is Best (*poems*)
The Meaningful Holiday (*poems*)

Pamphlets by Harvey Jackins

The Art of Listening
Co-Counseling for Married Couples
The Communication of Important Ideas
The Complete Appreciation of Oneself
The Distinctive Characteristics of Re-evaluation Counseling
The Enjoyment of Leadership
The Flexible Human in the Rigid Society
The Good and the Great in Art
How "Re-evaluation Counseling" Began
The Human Male—A Men's Liberation Draft Policy
Is Death Necessary?
Letter to a Respected Psychiatrist
The Logic of Being Completely Logical
Logical Thinking About a Future Society
The Nature of the Learning Process
The Necessity of Long Range Goals
A Rational Theory of Sexuality
The Uses of Beauty and Order
Where Did God Come From?
Who's In Charge?

Other Pamphlets

Aboriginal Australians Healing the Hurts of Racism
Accommodating Disability
All the Time in the World
Competition—An Inhuman Activity
Counseling on Early Sexual Memories
Creating a Just World: Leadership for the Twenty-First Century
Family Work
Guidelines for the Re-evaluation Counseling Communities
How Parents Can Counsel Their Children
How to Begin "Re-evaluation Counseling"
How to Give Children an Emotional Head Start
Internalized Racism
Introduction to Co-Counseling
Irish Liberation Policy
Language and Liberation—Information for RC Translators
The Liberation of Asians: Thinking About Asian Oppression and
    Liberation for People of Asian Heritage Living Outside of Asia
The Liberation of Men
Listening Effectively to Children
My Unity with All Women
Permit Their Flourishing
Primer for Clients (Humor)
Re-evaluation Counseling: A "Culturally Competent" Model for
    Social Liberation
The Re-evaluation Counseling Community
Re-evaluation Counseling: Social Implications
Re-evaluation Therapy: Theoretical Framework
Understanding and Supporting Young People
United to End Racism and the United Nations World Conference
    Against Racism: Durban, South Africa, August 2001
We Who Were Raised Poor: Ending the Oppression of Classism
What's Wrong with the "Mental Health" System and What Can
    Be Done About It
Why Lead in RC
Women
Working Together to End Racism: Healing from the Damage Caused
    by Racism

Some of the publications are available in Acholi/Luo, Afrikaans, Amharic,
Arabic, Basque, Chinese, Croatian, Czech, Danish, Dutch, Esperanto, Farsi,
Filipino, Finnish, French, German, Greek, Hebrew, Hungarian, Indonesian, Italian,
Japanese, Kannada, Kiswahili, Lithuanian, Malayalam, Marathi, Norwegian, Polish,
Portuguese, Romanian, Russian, Sami, Shona, Slovak, Spanish, Swedish, Tamil,
and Telugu.

Journals

Black Re-emergence — for everyone interested in black liberation
The Caring Parent — for everyone interested in parenting
Catholic Journal — for everyone interested in Catholic liberation
Classroom — a journal of the theory and practice of learning and
    educational change
Colleague — for communication among college and university faculty
Coming Home — for communication among owning-class people and their allies
Complete Elegance — for communication among disabled people and their allies
Creativity — a journal about art and artists and Re-evaluation Counseling
Forever and Ever — for exploring the possibility of physical immortality
Heritage — for information exchange on RC in Native American cultures
Men — for communication among men and their allies
Older and Bolder — for communication among older people and their allies
Our Asian Inheritance — for information exchange on RC in the Asian and
    Asian-heritage cultures
Our True Selves — for communication among middle-class people andtheir allies
Peace — for peace and disarmament activists
Pensamientos — for communication among people of Chicano/a ancestry
    and their allies
Present Time — for everybody; all about Re-evaluation Counseling
Raised-Poor Journal — for communication among raised-poor people and their allies
The RC Teacher — for those interested in the theory and practice of teaching RC
Recovery and Re-emergence — for those interested in "mental health" issues
Ruah Hadashah — for everyone interested in Jewish liberation
Seeds and Crystals — for poets and poetry lovers
Shuruk — for everyone interested in Arab liberation
Side by Side — for everyone interested in Lesbian/Gay/Bisexual liberation
Sisters — for everyone interested in women's liberation
Songs On Our Way Out — original songs with RC content
Transcendence — a journal about all kinds of religions and Re-evaluation Counseling
Well-Being — for exchange of information and ideas about health
Wide World Changing — for everyone interested in social change
Working For A Living — for everyone interested in working-class issues
Young and Powerful — for young people and young adults and everyone
    interested in their liberation

For price and order information, please contact:

RATIONAL ISLAND PUBLISHERS
P.O.BOX 2081, MAIN OFFICE STATION
SEATTLE, WASHINGTON 98111, USA
Tel. +1-206-284-0311
Fax +1-206-284-8429
email: litsales@rc.org